EMBROIDERY
FOR THE
HOME

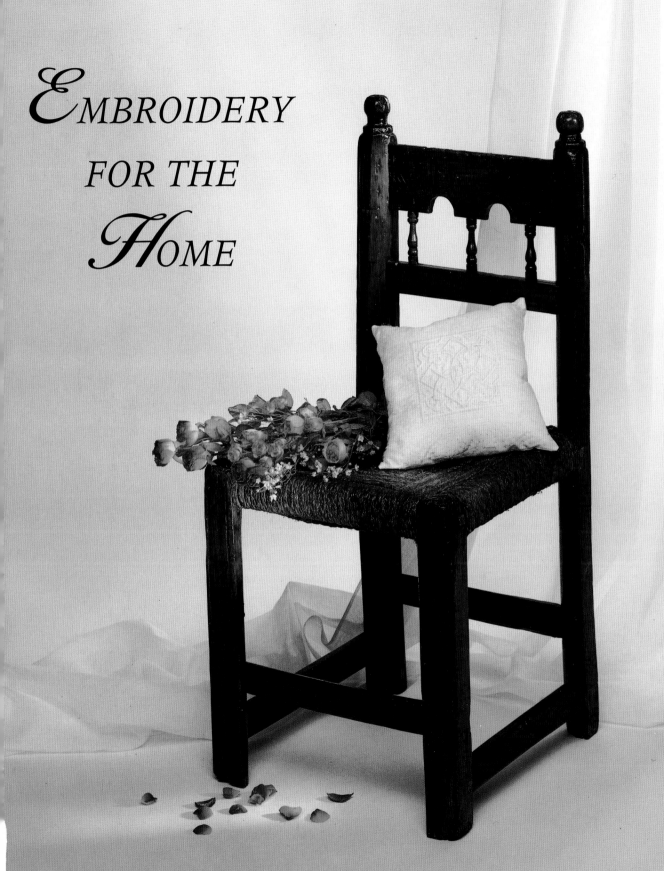

EMBROIDERY

FOR THE

HOME

Jenny Bullen

B.T. Batsford Ltd, London

Photography by KEITH TORRY

First published 1994

Typeset by Goodfellow and Egan Ltd, Cambridge and printed in Hong Kong

Published by
B.T. Batsford Ltd
4 Fitzhardinge Street
London W1H 0AH

British Library Cataloguing-in-Publication Data.
A catalogue record for this book is available from the British Library.

ISBN 0 7134 7107 7

CONTENTS

INTRODUCTION

The aim of this book is to introduce beginners to embroidery, therefore the projects are simple and easy to make and the techniques are quite basic. I have not included cross stitch, or other counted thread techniques, because there are many books available that cover this area of embroidery in detail. Rather, I have concentrated on easy surface stitchery, and included several quilting and appliqué techniques because they are extremely suitable for small items such as cushions, pillows and bags.

All the designs are simple; for some my inspiration was taken from flowers and nature, others are based on easy but effective techniques such as applied ribbons and shadow work. I have chosen a variety of sources for designs in the hopes that the book will provide you with a range of ideas and so encourage you to seek inspiration yourself in the world around you. Hopefully, you will learn to use and adapt your own ideas after working through some of the projects. Indeed, all of the designs included here can be used for other projects. The goose cushion, for example, could be extended into a child's quilt, and any of the flower designs could be used on a variety of household items such as cushions, tablecloths, napkins or photograph frames.

The first section of the book contains general instructions which relate to all the projects, and helpful advice is given on materials, transferring designs to fabric, stencilling, mounting and framing panels, and making cushions. Each project has a list of the materials required, although I have not been too specific about fabrics and threads because you may already have a supply that can be utilized, or you may wish to adapt the colours to suit your own scheme. If you are just beginning to embroider and you are not sure about the type of threads etc., your local craft or embroidery supplier will be able to offer you guidance.

The stitches I use are very simple, but infinitely adaptable – indeed the best stitches are usually the simplest. Stitch diagrams are given with each project and actual-size patterns are also shown where necessary. Do take care when cutting out your templates. It is worthwhile spending time on preparing accurate templates for your chosen design. It is also important to read through the instructions before beginning work on your project. Make sure you have prepared all your materials beforehand and do not be afraid to experiment a little with different coloured threads and fabrics.

I have enjoyed working on the embroideries in this book. Some of them require a sewing machine, but most of them are worked by hand. I hope you will find inspiration in these pages and feel encouraged to try out your needlework skills to create a whole range of beautiful embroidered items for your home.

GENERAL INSTRUCTIONS

This section contains some of the more general instructions relating to all the projects in the book. Where a technique relates specifically to one project, that technique is discussed under the project heading, e.g. quilting, which can be found on page 28 in the section on 'Butterflies'.

Materials and equipment

FABRICS

Fabrics for embroidery fall into three categories. Evenweave fabrics, such as cotton and cotton blends, have warp and weft threads of identical thicknesses and a perfectly regular weave. Plain weave describes any fabric that is woven and usually the embroidery design has to be transferred onto it as a guide for the stitchery. Canvas has a regular grid-like structure made up of stiffened warp and weft threads.

I have selected some of the finer plain weave and evenweave fabrics for making up the projects in this book, such as cotton, silk, calico, voile and sheer organza.

NEEDLES

A selection of sewing, quilting and embroidery needles will be needed.

For the hand embroidered projects I have used crewel needles of various sizes. These are of medium length with a sharp point and they are mainly used on finer plain weave fabrics.

Chenille needles are suitable for heavier fabrics; they are longer and thicker than crewel needles.

Tapestry needles are blunt-ended and are used on canvas and evenweave fabrics.

Quilting needles are sometimes also called 'betweens'. Compared to other needles, they are rather short and they have small, square eyes. Their length makes them ideal for hand quilting, which uses running stitch, because with practice it is possible to pick up several stitches at a time and to develop a regular, rhythmic working speed.

THREADS

A wide range of machine and hand embroidery threads are available in different colours and weights. Cotton, silk, linen, wool, metallic and synthetic threads can be found in abundance. Some are made up of several strands which can be separated for finer use, others cannot be divided.

I have used a mixture of machine and hand embroidery threads, as well as quilting threads and sewing cotton, for the projects illustrated in this book.

Embroidery threads are available in a variety of thicknesses and in many different colours. Cotton, silk, linen, wool, metallic and synthetic threads can all be used to create beautiful embroideries for the home.

(Previous page) This piece of embroidery illustrates several techniques. The outlines of the butterflies were drawn in gutta resist before the white habotai silk was hand-dyed with fabric paints. Free machine embroidery, couched metal threads and surface stitchery were used to give decoration and texture.

FRAMES

Many people prefer to work the embroidery without a frame. However, if the work is held tight it provides a good flat surface to stitch into and helps to keep the embroidery clean. It also avoids having to stretch the work after all the stitching has been done.

Small pieces of embroidery can be mounted in a ring, or tambour frame. This frame is made up of two rings that lock together and the fabric is carefully positioned between them. The fabric should always be pulled as taut as possible, but be sure not to distort the weave of the fabric. These frames are available in different sizes and they are easy to use.

Larger pieces of fabric will need to be mounted in a slate or square embroidery frame. I discuss how to prepare a larger piece of fabric for stitching on page 15.

Transferring designs to fabric

There are several ways of transferring designs to fabric, but the methods described here are suitable for the designs shown in this book.

(Right)
Small pieces of embroidery can be mounted in a ring, or tambour frame. Larger pieces need to be mounted in a slate or square frame.

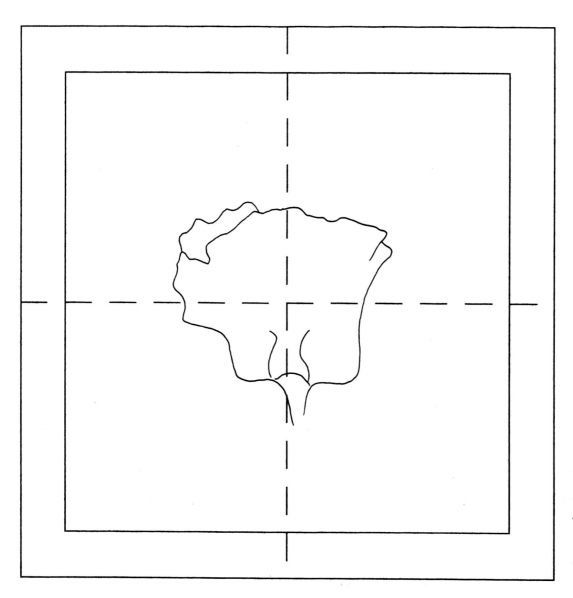

Fig.1
Simple tracing method. Place the paper with the traced drawing on a flat surface and lay the fabric over the top, matching centres if necessary. Using a sharp pencil, trace the design on to the fabric.

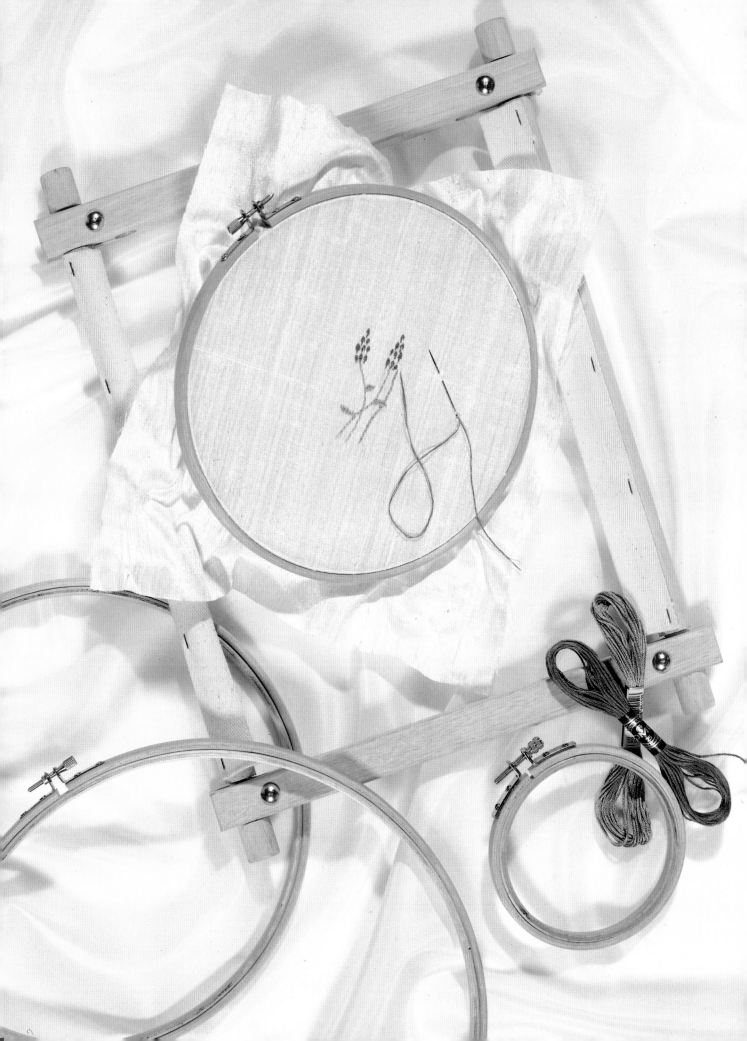

SIMPLE TRACING

Some of the designs can be worked on sheer fabrics and if you decide to do this it is usually possible to trace the design directly onto the fabric.

1 Using a black felt tip pen, trace off the lines of the design onto greaseproof or tracing paper.
2 Lay the tracing, face up, on a flat surface and secure with strips of masking tape.
3 Place the fabric over the design and secure with masking tape. In some instances, it is necessary to find the centre of the fabric first. Carefully fold the fabric in half lengthways and mark the fold with a line of tacking stitches. Repeat with the width of the fabric and carefully centre these lines over the centre of the drawing (see Figure 1). If it is difficult to see the design lines, the paper could be secured with tape against a window and the fabric placed over it.
4 Using a sharp, fine H or HB pencil, lightly trace the design on to the fabric. Do not press too heavily. You will find that, as you sew, most of the pencil lines will wear off. Soluble pens (the line dissolves when painted with cold water) may be used, but the lines often return after they have been washed away and these pens should therefore be used

Fig.2
Tracing and tacking method. Lay the drawing over the fabric and tack through both layers using small running stitches. Carefully tear away the tracing.

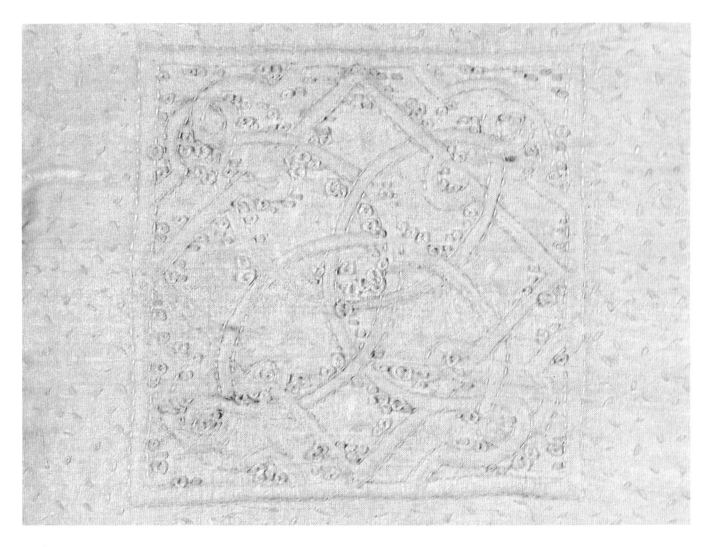

with great caution. A water soluble coloured pencil is an alternative method of marking.

TRACING AND TACKING

Designs worked on opaque fabric can all be transferred in this way.

1 Using greaseproof paper, trace off the lines of the design with a sharp HB pencil.
2 Pin the paper pattern over the fabric, centring the fabric as described on page 12, if necessary. Tack the layers together.
3 Using small running stitches, carefully outline all the lines of the design (see Figure 2). Make sure that all the threads are securely fastened.

4 When all the lines have been worked, carefully tear away the paper to reveal the stitched outline of the design. Work the embroidery, removing the tacking stitches as you work.

Making a stencil

Stencils are an excellent method of colouring plain fabrics when a definite outline is required, e.g. a flower or a butterfly. A sheet of strong card can be used if the stencil is to be used only once or twice. However, it is advisable to buy a sheet of oiled stencil card (available from art and craft shops) if you intend to use it several times.

1 Using tracing paper, trace off the outline of the design and transfer it to

The tracing and tacking method was used to create this design which was transferred on to the herb pillow on page 68. The embroidery is worked in a technique called Italian quilting, with some added hand stitches.

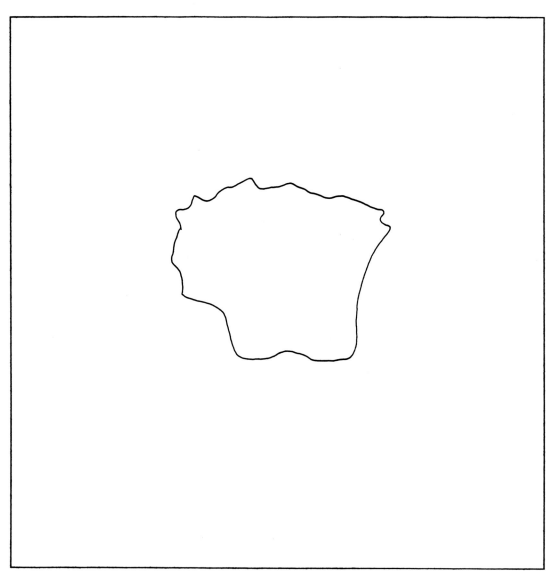

(Below)
This poppy design was stencilled on to the calico workbag which can be found on page 83. The petals are outlined in matching red thread using machine embroidery; the stem and base of each flower are worked in the same way.

the centre of the card. Using a sharp craft knife, carefully cut around the design.

2 Lay the fabric face up on a flat surface and position the stencil on top of the fabric. To apply the colour to the fabric, use a stencil brush, a diffuser (both available from art and craft shops) or spatter with an old toothbrush dipped in fabric paint. (Remember to use rubber gloves for this.)

Alternatively, use a sponge dipped lightly into the fabric paint and applied sparingly to the fabric.

3 Leave the fabric to dry thoroughly before removing the stencil. Iron the back of the cloth to set the fabric paint.

Preparing the fabric for stitching

If you are working a small piece of embroidery, mount it in a ring or tambour frame (see page 10). Larger pieces of work need to be mounted in a slate or square frame. The frame can accommodate a reasonable length of fabric, which can be rolled around the rollers at each end.

1 First, mark the centres of the two strips of webbing on each of the rollers attached to the frame, as well as the centres of your chosen fabric.
2 Turn under the raw edges of the fabric and machine, or handsew in place. Pin the fabric to the webbing on the top and bottom rollers, matching the centres.
3 Working from the centres outwards, and using a strong thread, oversew the two opposite sides of the fabric to the strips of webbing.
4 Slot the side bars in place. If the fabric is longer than the side bars, it will be necessary to carefully roll the excess fabric around the bars at each end of the frame.
5 When this has been done, pull the frame so that the fabric is as taut as possible, taking care not to tear the fabric. Slot the pegs in the appropriate holes. Many of the frames available today have wing nuts instead of holes, in which case follow the instructions given and simply tighten the wing nuts when the fabric has been pulled as tight as possible. Guidelines for mounting work in these roller frames are usually provided with the frame when it is purchased.
6 Using a very strong linen or similar thread, or fine string, lace the fabric to the side bars. You are now ready to start your embroidery.

Stretching embroidery

Most of the small embroideries in this book will not need to be stretched when they have been worked. A light press with a moderate steam iron on the wrong side of the work will suffice.

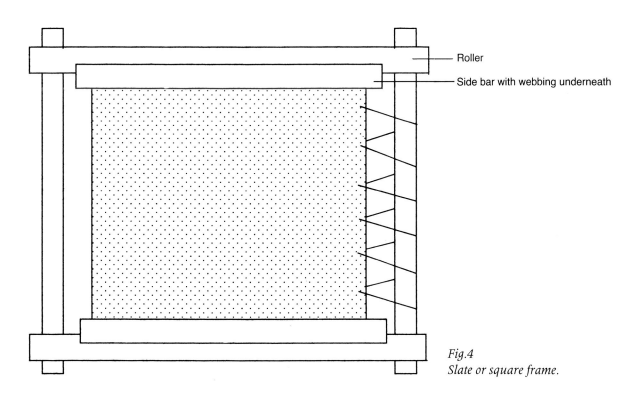

Roller

Side bar with webbing underneath

Fig.4
Slate or square frame.

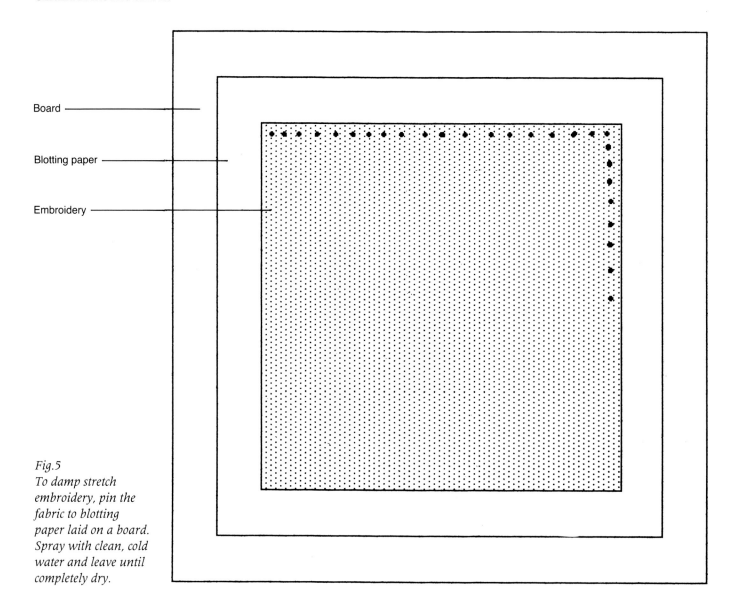

Board ————

Blotting paper ————

Embroidery ————

Fig.5
To damp stretch embroidery, pin the fabric to blotting paper laid on a board. Spray with clean, cold water and leave until completely dry.

However, some of the larger pieces of work may become distorted whilst being stitched and these will need to be dampened and stretched when they have been removed from the frame.

1 Cover a board with several layers of absorbent paper, such as blotting paper.
2 Lay the embroidery face up on the paper. Using drawing pins, carefully pin the embroidery to the board, working around the edges of the fabric, and keeping the grain of the fabric straight and the work as taut as possible.
3 Spray the work with clean, cold water (a plastic spray bottle obtainable

in garden centres is ideal for this). Leave the work to dry before removing the drawing pins. If the fabric has become very distorted it may be necessary to repeat the procedure in order to bring it back to its original shape.

The piece of embroidered fabric can now be made up into panels, cushions, or any of the other projects shown in this book. In the following pages I give general instructions on mounting and framing panels, making up cushions and simple ways of creating cards and tassels. These methods can be applied to any of the embroideries in the book.

Mounting and framing panels

If the embroidery is to be used as a picture to be displayed or hung on the wall, it should be mounted over very strong card.

The embroidery can, of course, be mounted and framed by professional picture framers, but this can be quite expensive. However, most framers will make up a frame to the required size and the work can be put together at home, which will reduce the cost.

1 Establish the exact size that the finished panel is to be and cut a piece of strong card to this measurement. It is

A finished embroidery mounted and framed. Instructions for this machine embroidered poppy panel can be found on page 88.

quite useful to tack this measurement around the edge of the embroidered fabric before starting.

2 After pressing or stretching the embroidery, lay the work face down on a clean, flat surface and place the card on top, lining up the edges of the card with the rows of tacking stitches.

3 Using a strong linen thread or fine string, lace the two opposite sides of the work over the back of the card, beginning at the centre and working out to the sides. Carefully fold in the corners so that they are hidden from the front. Repeat with the two other sides.

4 If you are using a purchased frame, as suggested for some of the work in this book, the picture framer will probably also supply a backing board and hooks. Slip the frame over the mounted panel and place the backing board over the back of the work. Hold in place with adhesive tape. Insert the hooks in the back of the frame and add a piece of strong cord to hang the panel.

Fig.6
Establish the exact size that the finished panel is to be and tack this measurement around the edge of the embroidered fabric.

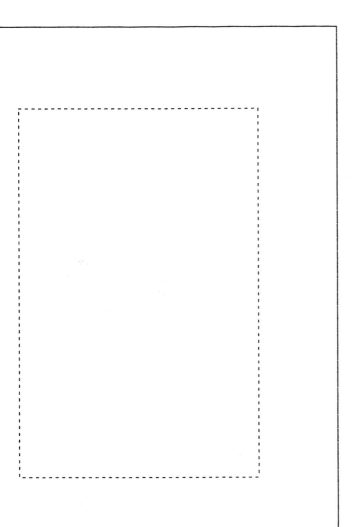

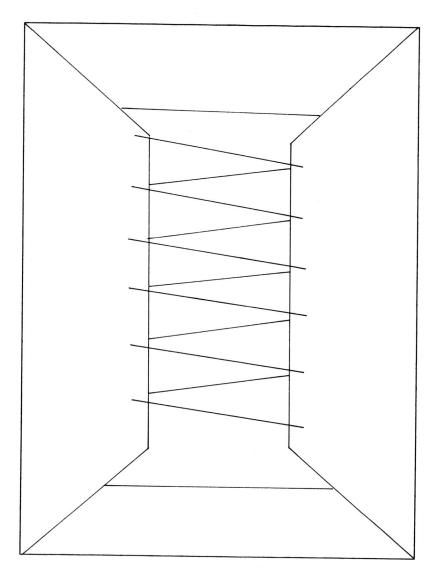

must be placed in boiling water for several minutes and then left to dry.

The piping cord is usually covered with fabric and this fabric should always be cut on the bias (see instructions on page 19 on how to make a continuous bias strip) You should allow for this when buying your fabric. The width of the bias strip will depend on the thickness of the cord, but it should be wide enough to surround the cord and give a good seam allowance.

1 Decide on the length of the cord and place it in the centre of the bias strip; fold the strip in half lengthways and tack in place. Stitch in place, as close to the cord as possible (see Figure 8).
2 To use as an edging, on a cushion or bag for example, sandwich the fabric-covered piping cord between the right side of the fabric and the lining, with all the raw edges meeting.

Fig.7
Using a strong thread, lace the sides of the work over the back of the card, beginning at the centre and working out to the sides. Carefully fold in the corners so that they are hidden from the front.

Cushions

I have included several cushion projects: a herb pillow with an embroidered design taken from an early English knot garden, a Celtic cushion, a quilted cushion decorated with printed gold stars, and others. These instructions will help you make up the various cushions throughout the book.

PIPED CORDS

A piped cord to trim cushions or a quilt is not really difficult to make. Piping cord can be bought in different thicknesses. If it is not pre-shrunk, it

Detail of the bolster cushion on page 47. The piping is worked around the two cushion ends in matching floral fabric.

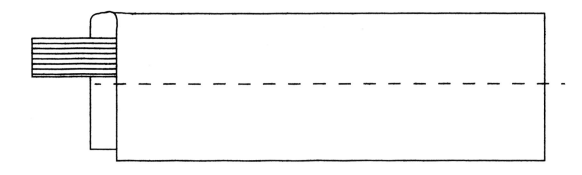

Fig.9
With all the raw edges meeting, pin, tack and stitch the layers together.

3 Pin and tack the piped cord in place (see Figure 9). When turning corners, pin the piping into place, taking care not to distort the cord. Machine stitch as close as possible to the piping. Neaten the seam and turn the fabric to the right side.

4 To join lengths of cord together, first of all unpick the bias strip on both sides. Trim the cord so that there is an overlap of about 2.5 cm (1 in) and unravel them for that length. Piping cord is usually three cords twisted together; on one end trim away two pieces of cord and on the other side one piece. Twist the remaining pieces together, secure carefully with thread and recover the cord with fabric.

A CONTINUOUS BIAS STRIP

1 Cut a square of fabric and fold it in half diagonally. Cut the fabric along the diagonal line, AB (see Figure 10).

2 With rights sides together, pin the edges AD to CB. Stitch the seam together and press open.

3 Using a ruler and pencil, mark the

19

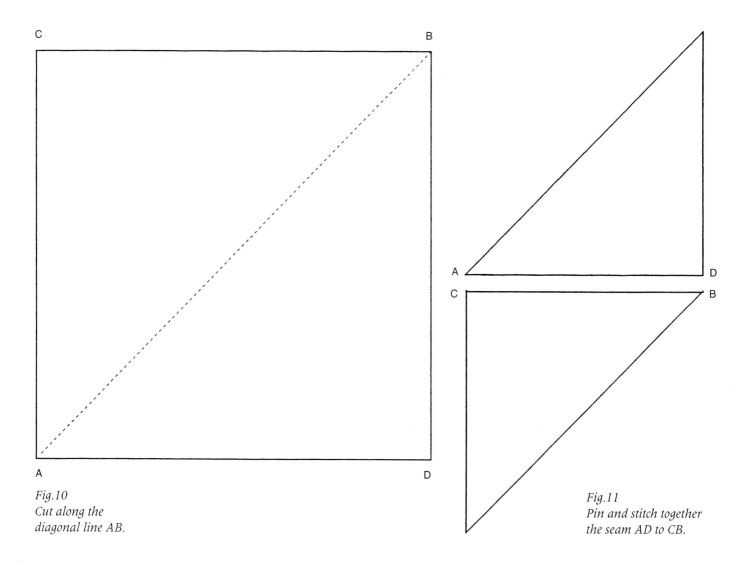

*Fig.10
Cut along the
diagonal line AB.*

*Fig.11
Pin and stitch together
the seam AD to CB.*

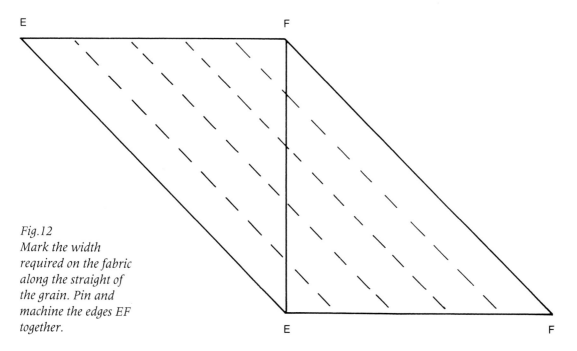

*Fig.12
Mark the width
required on the fabric
along the straight of
the grain. Pin and
machine the edges EF
together.*

width you require in strips on the fabric, along the straight grain (see Figure 12).

4 With right sides together, bring the edges EF together and pin and machine the seam, remembering to drop it the width of one bias strip.

5 Begin cutting the strips at one end and a continuous strip of fabric will be formed.

MAKING UP CUSHIONS

When buying a pad for a cushion, remember to choose one that is larger than the finished size of the cushion. The zip for the opening should be approximately 4 cm (1½ in) smaller than the finished cushion.

1 Cut out the cushion front with 1.5 cm (½ in) seam allowances. If you intend to insert a zip opening, the fabric for the back of the cushion should be in two pieces, each with a seam allowance.

2 To insert the zip, place the cushion backs right sides together and stitch a 2 cm (¾ in) seam at either end. Insert the zip into the opening. Make sure that the zip is open before making up the cushion.

3 Place back and front of cushion right sides together and pin and tack in place. Insert the piping cord if required. Machine around all four sides, trim the seams and turn the cushion to the right side. Insert the cushion pad.

4 If you do not intend to insert a zip and simply slip stitch the cushion opening together, pin and machine stitch around three sides only. Turn the cushion to the right side and slip stitch the opening together after inserting the cushion pad. The slip stitches can easily be removed and the cushion pad taken out when the cushion cover needs washing.

An alternative method to a zipped or slip-stitched opening is an envelope type back opening:

1 For the cushion back, cut two pieces of fabric, each the same measurement as the width of the cushion, but three quarters of the length.

2 Turn under and machine stitch a narrow hem along the width of one piece. Repeat with the other.

3 With right sides together, place one cushion back over the front of the cushion. Pin and tack in place.

4 Pin and tack the second piece over the first one so that they overlap in the middle.

5 Machine around all four sides of the cushion. Neaten the seams and turn the cushion to the right side.

Cords and tassels

A twisted cord to trim cushions, or to use as draw strings, can be made simply and cheaply. It is much more successful if two people can be involved in making it.

1 Cut lengths of yarn approximately three times longer than the required

Fig.13
With right sides together, place one cushion back over the front of the cushion. Pin and tack in place. Pin and tack the second piece over the first one so that they overlap and machine around all four sides of the cushion.

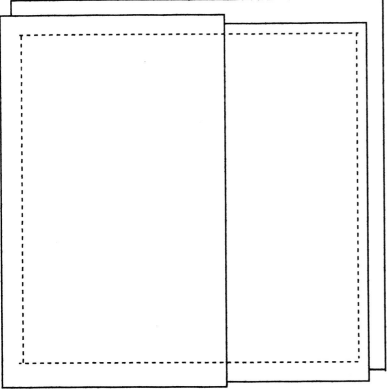

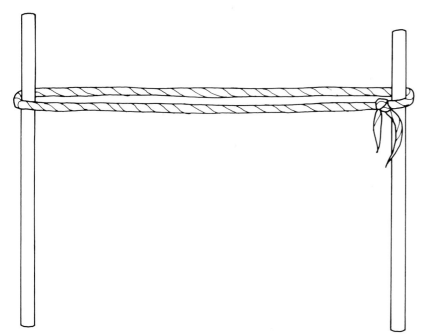

A quick and easy cord can be made on the sewing machine using a firm string or twine as a base and covering it with machine embroidery threads. Set the machine at its widest swing, with a closely set stitch. Place the string under the foot and stitch down the length. It may be necessary to repeat the procedure to closely cover the string.

TASSELS

Tassels can also be made very simply and cheaply and can be used to trim cushions or bags.

1 Cut a piece of card to the required length of the tassel and wind thread around it until it is the required thickness.
2 Cut a separate length of yarn. Thread through the loops at one edge of the card and tie them together.
3 Remove the yarn from the card, then cut a second length of yarn and tie the yarn from the card together, about 2 cm (¾ in) from the looped end.
4 Cut through all the loops at the other end of the tassel.

Fig.14
To make a twisted cord, knot the ends into a loop and insert a pencil in either end. Twist the pencils in opposite directions until the threads are tightly twisted together.

finished length of the cord. Use a good quality thread.
2 Knot the ends into loops. Insert a pencil in either end and pull on the yarn until it is quite taut.
3 Keeping a good tension, twist the pencils in opposite directions, until the threads are tightly twisted together.
4 Remove the pencils; fold the cord in half and it will twist itself together.

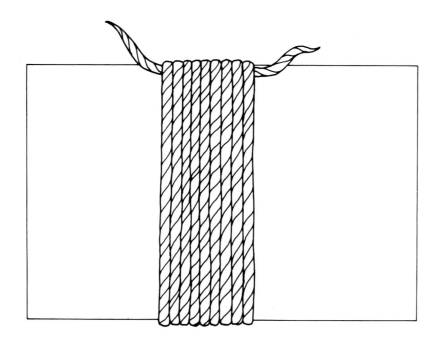

Fig.15
To make a tassel wind the thread around a piece of card. Cut a separate length of yarn, thread through the loops at one end of the card and tie them together.

(Left)
A twisted cord is used as a draw string on this small pot pourri bag (for instructions on how to make the bag, see page 114).

BUTTERFLIES

Butterflies, with their beautiful shapes and colours, provided the inspiration for the panel and slippers in this section.

PANEL

A collection of butterflies provided the inspiration for this small panel which was embroidered in fine silk threads using a combination of simple stitches and gold fabric paint. Although the panel illustrated here is quite small, 16.5 × 11.5 cm (6½ × 4½ in), it could be made larger by adding more butterflies. Arrange them in rows to retain the effect of a collection of butterflies, but make the panels as large as you want.

Materials
- Background fabric: natural, slubbed silk
- Tracing paper
- Gold fabric paint
- Assortment of fine embroidery threads (in this case fine silk threads were used but one strand of stranded embroidery cotton could be used instead)
- Card or oiled stencil card
- Sponge or stencil brush
- Craft knife
- Strong card for backing
- Purchased frame

Fig.16
To make a stencil trace around the outlines of the butterflies shown here and transfer the designs to a piece of card or oiled stencil card.

(Right)
Cream coloured silks and blue and purple embroidery threads are used for the panel and the slippers. Gold fabric paint is applied to the panel before the embroidery is worked and simple stitches are used on both designs.

METHOD

I used a stencil to transfer the butterfly design on to the background fabric

1 To make the stencil, use greaseproof paper or tracing paper to trace around the outlines of the butterflies in Figure 16 and transfer the design on to a piece of card or oiled stencil card. Remember to leave plenty of card around the shape of each butterfly or it will be difficult to apply the fabric paint. Using a sharp craft knife carefully cut around each outline.

2 Lay the background fabric right side up on a flat surface and place the largest stencil in the top left hand corner (see Figure 17).

3 Using either a dry sponge or a stencil brush, lightly dab gold fabric paint through the stencil. Make sure the paint is completely dry before lifting away the stencil. Repeat the procedure with the other stencils, arranging the butterflies as illustrated on page 27, or choose your own arrangement.

4 To set the gold paint, iron the back of the fabric. It will be easier to work the embroidery if, at this stage, the fabric is mounted in a hoop or a small frame (see General Instructions on page 10.)

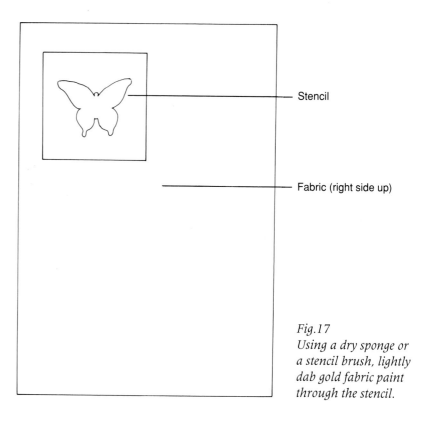

Stencil

Fabric (right side up)

Fig.17
Using a dry sponge or a stencil brush, lightly dab gold fabric paint through the stencil.

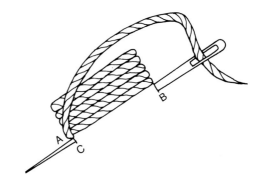

Fig.19
Satin stitch. *Bring the needle out of the fabric at A, and re-insert it at B. Bring the needle out again at C, which should be very close to the previous stitch.*

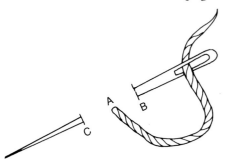

Fig.18
Back stitch. *Bring the needle out of the ground fabric at A. Take it through to the back of the fabric at B and bring out again at C, forming a continuous line of stitches.*

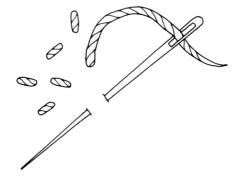

Fig.20
Seeding stitch. *A very simple and effective filling stitch consisting of tiny back stitches worked in every direction.*

The butterfly wings and antennae are outlined in back stitch and satin stitch, and the bodies are embroidered in satin stitch. The gold paint is allowed to peep through the embroidered areas, which adds to the charm of the design.

5 The embroidery is worked in very simple stitches. Some of the wings and the antennae are outlined in back stitch (see Figure 18); the bodies are embroidered in satin stitch (see Figure 19), which is a traditional filling stitch. On the two larger butterflies, areas of the wings near the bodies are worked in seeding stitch (see Figure 20) with outer sections of the wings worked in satin stitch. However, these are only suggestions and you could substitute any of your favourite embroidery stitches. On the smaller butterflies the embroidered areas are worked in satin stitch. Do not be tempted to completely cover all the butterflies with stitchery as part of the charm of the design lies in the way areas of gold paint are revealed.
6 When all the embroidery has been worked cut a piece of backing card to fit the frame and mount the work over the card (see General Instructions on page 17).

SLIPPERS

A different butterfly has been used to decorate a pair of lightweight travelling slippers. These are worked in silk with a lightly quilted sole. However, a layer of thick felt could be incorporated in the sole if the slippers are required to be slightly more hardwearing.

If you have not tried any quilting before, read through the following section which explains the techniques, before starting to make the slippers.

QUILTING

English, or wadded, quilting is a sandwich of two fabrics with a layer of wadding between. Smooth, slightly shiny fabrics are suitable for the top fabric, such as silk, satin, cotton or polyester cotton blends. A synthetic 2 oz wadding is a good, general purpose wadding. Muslin can be used for the backing, although any fine, smooth fabric could be used. If the item is to be double-sided, a more substantial fabric than muslin should be used.

Any fine sewing thread can be used, although a specific quilting thread is

now available in a wide range of colours. Traditionally, the colour of the thread should match the ground fabric. Quilting needles are fairly short and they should be quite fine. If the thread is run through beeswax before stitching, it will strengthen it and help to prevent it from knotting.

Transferring the design to fabric

If the design is simple, the easiest method of transferring it to the fabric is to make a template from thin card. If the fabric is dark in colour, lay the template on the surface and trace lightly around it with a hard pencil, or a water soluble coloured pencil. Alternatively, for light fabrics place the fabric directly over the design and trace over it with a pencil.

Where designs are more complicated, the tracing and tacking method can be used (see General Instructions on page 13).

Preparing the fabrics

Good preparation is essential for quilting or the layers of fabric will slip and be very difficult to handle.

1 Cut out the backing fabric slightly larger than you intend the finished piece of work to be, as the quilting will shrink the fabrics. Press the fabric well and lay it on a flat surface.
2 Cut out the wadding to the same size as the backing fabric and smooth carefully over it.
3 Cut out the top fabric and press well. Place it over the wadding and smooth into place.
4 Starting from the centre tack a horizontal and vertical line of stitches, carefully smoothing the fabrics into place. Then make a grid of stitches over the whole area, approximately 8–10 cm (3–4 in) apart (see Figure 21). Finally, tack around the outside edge of the fabric sandwich.

English, or wadded quilting: a layer of wadding is sandwiched between silk and a backing fabric.

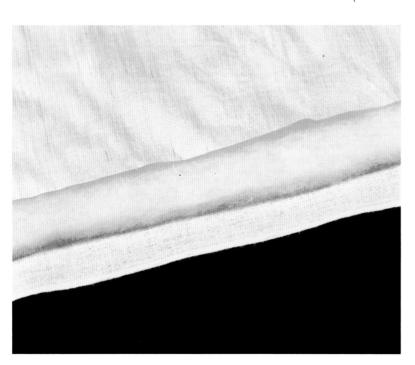

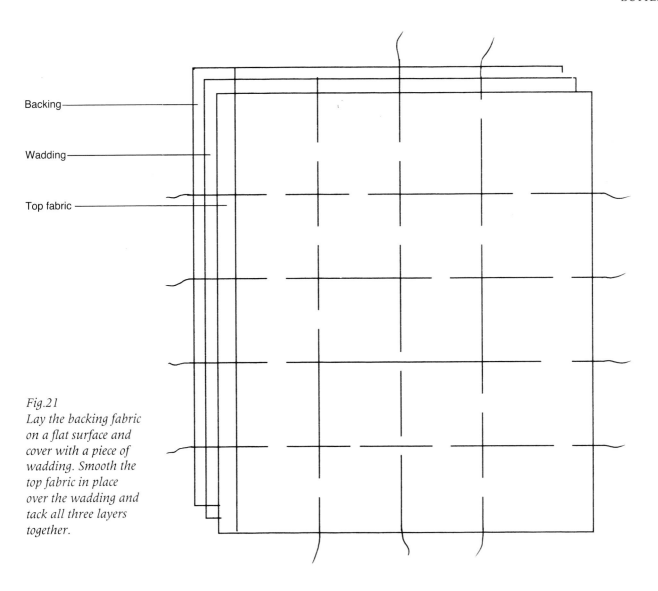

Backing ——————

Wadding ——————

Top fabric ——————

Fig.21
Lay the backing fabric on a flat surface and cover with a piece of wadding. Smooth the top fabric in place over the wadding and tack all three layers together.

5 Running stitch is most often used for quilting because it is quite fast (see Figure 22). However, other stitches such as back stitch are very successful, although not very suitable for large items such as quilts because they would take so long to stitch. The quilted surface can be decorated with seeding and french knots, beads and sequins.

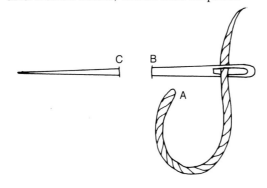

Fig.22
Running stitch.
Bring the needle out of the fabric at A, insert it at B and bring out again at C.

Materials for slippers

- 50 cm (½ yd) silk
- 50 cm (½ yd) 2 oz terylene wadding
- 25 cm (¼ yd) calico
- Embroidery or quilting thread
- Tracing or greaseproof paper

METHOD

1 Trace off the pattern for the slipper uppers on to a piece of thin card (see Figure 23). Cut out the shape and place it on the silk fabric. Draw lightly around the template with a hard pencil, but do not cut out the uppers yet as the quilting will shrink the fabric. Reverse

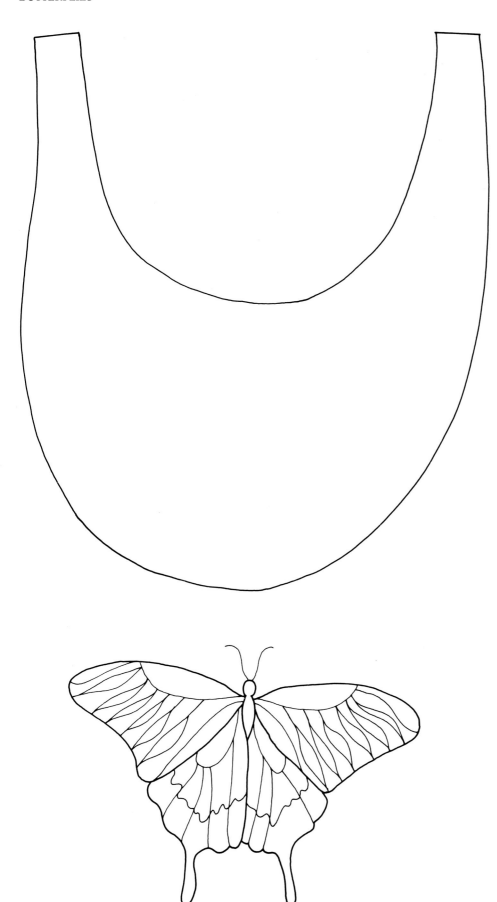

Fig.23
Trace off the pattern on to a piece of paper or thin card. Cut out the shape, place it on the fabric and outline it. Repeat for the second slipper, remembering to reverse the template.

Fig.24
Butterfly design for slippers.

the paper pattern for the other slipper and repeat the process.

2 Using tracing or greaseproof paper trace off the pattern for the butterfly (see Figure 24) and transfer it to each of the slipper uppers (see General Instructions on page 13).

3 Prepare the fabrics (silk, wadding and calico) for quilting as outlined in the Quilting section on page 28.

4 Quilt the butterfly shapes using back stitch. A contrasting coloured thread was used for the slippers, but a self-coloured thread could be used if desired.

5 When all the quilting has been worked, place the pattern for the uppers over the silk again and redraw the outline if necessary. Cut out both upper shapes, and then two more shapes from the silk fabric for the lining. Pin the layers together.

6 Cut a bias strip (see page 19) from the silk fabric (enough to bind the uppers and around the soles of the slippers).

7 With the right sides together, pin a length of bias strip to the inner edge of each upper (see Figure 25). Machine through all the layers, turn the bias strip to the wrong side and hem it in place (see Figure 26).

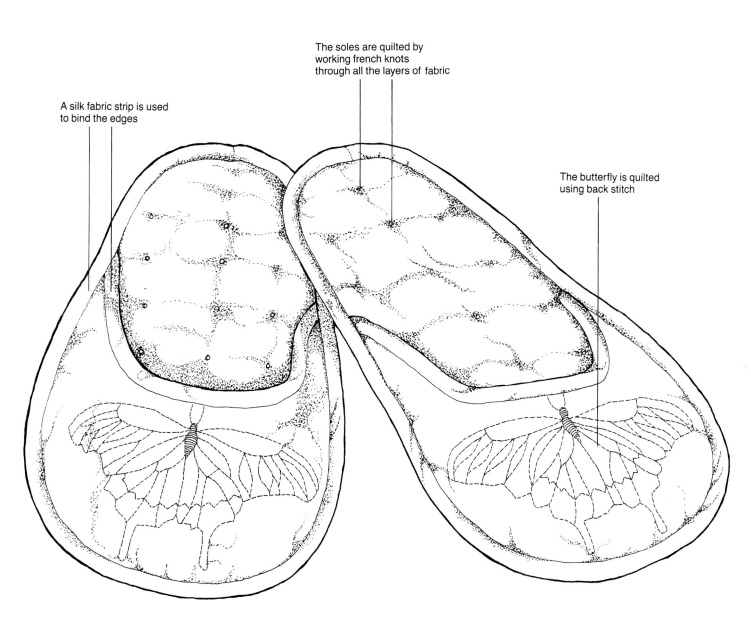

The soles are quilted by working french knots through all the layers of fabric

A silk fabric strip is used to bind the edges

The butterfly is quilted using back stitch

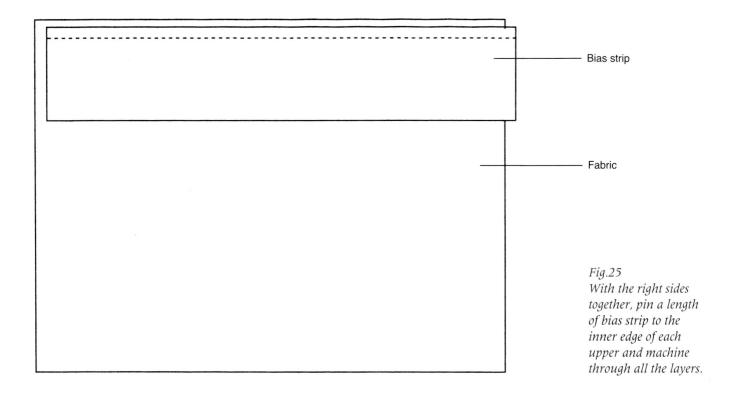

Fig.25
With the right sides together, pin a length of bias strip to the inner edge of each upper and machine through all the layers.

Bias strip

Fabric

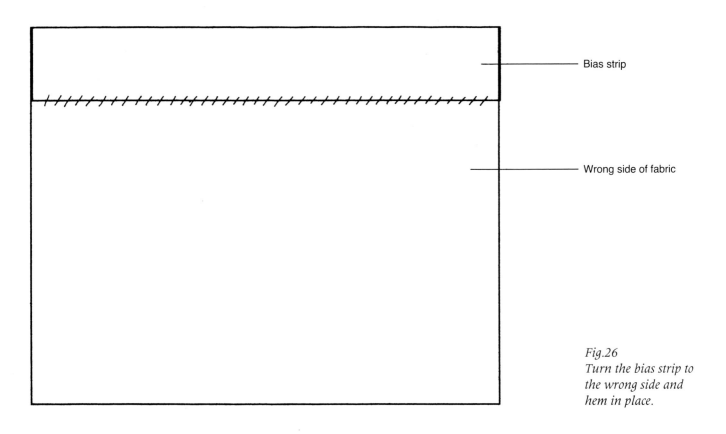

Fig.26
Turn the bias strip to the wrong side and hem in place.

Bias strip

Wrong side of fabric

8 Trace off the pattern for the sole of the slippers (see Figure 28). (A more accurate pattern will be obtained by drawing around your own foot.) Draw lightly around the outline on the silk fabric, remembering to reverse the pattern when cutting out the second sole. Do not cut out the shapes yet.

9 Make a sandwich of calico, wadding and silk, as for the uppers.

10 To quilt the soles, work french knots through all the layers of fabric, 2.5 cm (1 in) apart, this time in a self-coloured thread (see Figure 27).

11 Place the patterns for the soles on the silk and redraw the outlines if necessary. Cut out each sole. Cut out two extra patterns in calico for the sole, and also in felt if required.

12 Sandwich all the layers together and tack them in place.

13 Matching each sole to the correct upper, pin and tack the uppers in place.

14 Pin and tack a bias strip around the sole. Machine in place and trim the raw edges before turning the bias strip over and hemming in place.

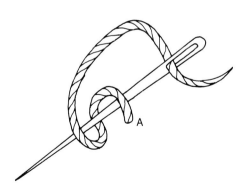

Fig.27
French knot. *Bring the needle to the front of the fabric at A. Twist the thread once around the needle and re-insert in almost the same place.*

*Fig.28
Pattern for the slipper sole. Remember to reverse the pattern when tracing the second foot.*

GEESE

The design for the goose cushion was adapted from the greetings card I discovered in a craft shop in Holland. The geese on the cushion are appliquéd on to a blue cotton background, whereas the goose on the card is hand-embroidered.

CUSHION

The cushion front is quilted after the squares are stitched together. Instead of a zip opening, the cushion is made up rather like a pillow case and ties are added. The finished size is 40 × 40 cm (16 × 16 in)

METHOD

1 Cut out four squares of blue cotton fabric, 17 × 17 cm (6¾ × 6¾ in).
2 Using tracing paper, trace off the two goose patterns (see Figures 29 and 30).

Materials

- 50 cm (½ yard) metre blue and white striped cotton fabric
- Square of plain blue cotton fabric, 35 × 35 cm (14 × 14 in)
- Small piece of white cotton fabric
- Yellow and black embroidery threads
- White sewing cotton
- Blue quilting thread
- Square of wadding, 40 × 40 cm (16 × 16 in)
- Square of butter muslin for quilting, 40 × 40 cm (16 × 16 in)
- Cushion pad, 40 × 40 cm (16 × 16 in)

Blue and white fabrics complement the goose design which is used here on a cushion for a child's nursery.

Pin each pattern to the white cotton fabric and, using small running stitches, carefully outline the lines of the design. Follow the instructions on page 13 (Tracing and tacking) and cut two geese from each of the patterns, so that two of the geese are facing in the opposite direction. Carefully cut out each goose, remembering to leave a 5 mm (¼ in) seam allowance.
3 Carefully turn under and tack the seam allowance on each goose. It will be necessary to snip into the seam allowance in some places where the curves fall, but do this very sparingly. Press each piece.
4 Centre a goose on each square of blue fabric; pin and tack in place.
5 Using matching sewing cotton, hem stitch each goose in position (see Figure 31). Remove all the tacking threads.
6 Using a yellow embroidery thread, add feet and beaks in straight stitches. Embroider a french knot (see Figure 27) in black thread for the eyes.
7 If the geese are to be applied using a sewing machine follow steps 1 and 2 above, but cut them out without any seam allowances. Pin and tack them to the blue squares. Use a fairly wide zig-zag stitch and a matching sewing thread to stitch them down. Embroider the feet and beaks by hand as instructed.

8 To make up the cushion front, cut two strips of blue and white striped fabric 4.5 cm (1¾ in) wide and 17 cm (6¾ in) long.

9 With right sides together, pin and machine stitch a strip of fabric to the base of one of the blue squares. Then, with right sides together, pin and

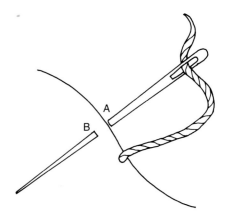

Fig.31
Hem stitch. *Take the needle through the ground fabric only at A. Bring it out at B through all the layers of fabric. Use a matching coloured thread and make the stitches as small as possible.*

The goose design is traced on to white cotton fabric and hem stitched on to the blue background fabric. Using yellow embroidery thread and straight stitches the beak and feet are added; a french knot is worked for the eye.

Figs.29, 30 Trace the outline of the geese on to tracing or greaseproof paper.

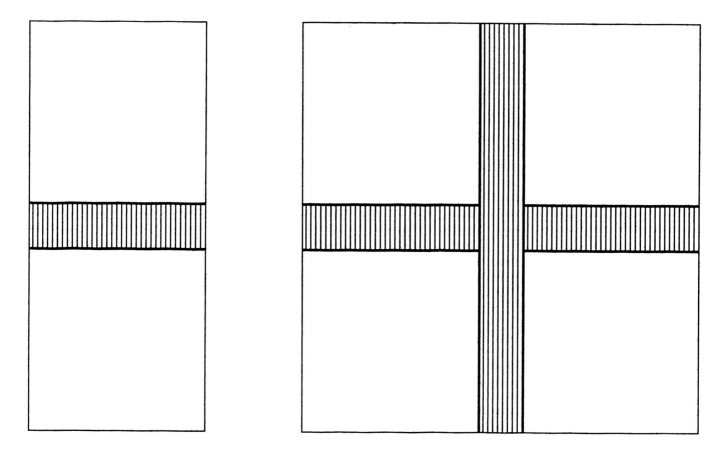

Fig.32 (top left)
Pin and machine
stitch a strip of striped
fabric to the base of a
square. Pin and
machine the opposite
side of the strip to the
top of a second blue
square.

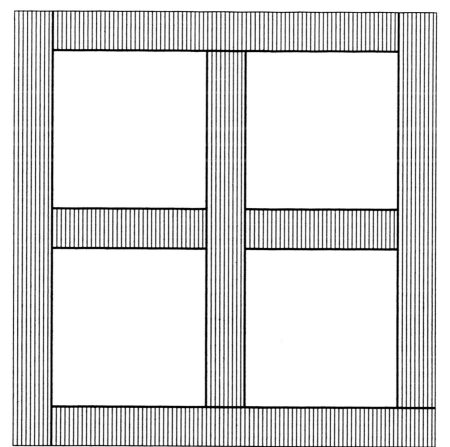

Fig.33 (top right)
Join the two sets of
squares together with
a long strip of striped
fabric.

Fig.34 (right)
For the border sew
a strip of blue and
white fabric to two
opposite sides of the
square. Repeat with
the remaining two
sides.

machine stitch the opposite side of the strip to the top of a second blue square. Press the seams. Repeat this procedure with the other two squares.

10 With right sides together, pin, tack and machine one strip of striped fabric 35 cm (13½ in) to a long side of one set of squares. Stitch the opposite side of the strip to the other set of squares.

11 Make a border by sewing two strips of blue and white fabric, each 41 cm (16¼ in) long, to two opposite sides of the square, and then repeat with the remaining two sides, each 36 cm (14¼ in) long. Press the cushion well.

12 To quilt the cushion, lay the muslin on a flat surface and cover with the wadding. Lay the cushion front right side up over the wadding. Tack all the layers together.

13 Quilt with tiny running stitches around each goose and around the edge of each blue square. Refer to the section on Quilting (see page 28), for more detailed instructions.

14 To make up the cushion, from the blue and white fabric cut eight strips 30 cm (11½ in) long and 5 cm (2 in) wide for the ties. Cut a piece of fabric 43 × 18 cm (17 × 7 in) for the facing and a piece 61 × 43 cm (24 × 17 in) for the cushion backing. Check your own cushion measurements carefully before you cut out these last two fabrics, as the

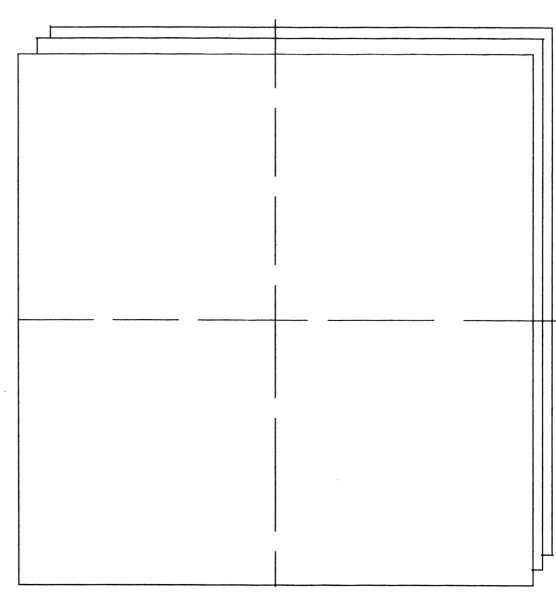

Fig.35
Lay the muslin on a flat surface, cover with the wadding and lay the cushion right side up over the wadding. Tack all the layers together.

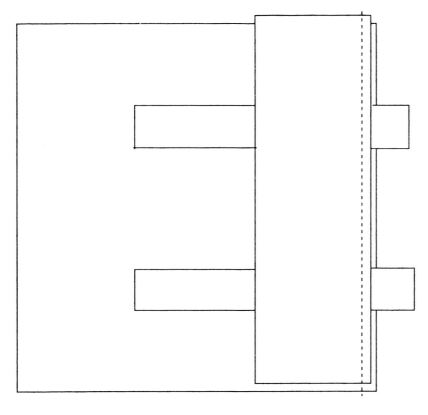

17 Turn under and machine stitch a narrow hem on one long edge of the facing strip.

18 With right sides together, place the long, unstitched edge of the facing to the cushion opening. Pin and machine the seam, ensuring that the ties are sewn into place at the same time.

19 Turn under and machine stitch a narrow hem on one long edge of the facing strip.

20 Place the front, front facing and back of the cushion right sides together with the two stitched edges on the same side. Pin, tack and machine around three sides, leaving open the facing side. Trim the seams and turn the cushion to the right side. Turn and press the facings to the wrong side. Insert the cushion pad and secure the cushion with the ties.

Fig.36
Place the long, unstitched edge of the facing to the cushion opening. Pin and machine the seam, ensuring that the ties are sewn into place at the same time.

(Right)
The cushion is secured with matching ties.

quilting will slightly shrink the fabrics and may alter the fabric requirements.

15 For the ties, with right sides together pin two of the narrow strips together and machine around three sides leaving a narrow side open. Turn the tie to the wrong side and press carefully. Machine along the sides, close to the edge. Repeat for the other three ties.

16 Tack two of the ties to the front side opening and two ties to the back, centring them carefully so that they will match up when the cushion is finally completed.

GREETINGS CARD

The greetings card was purchased with an aperture cut in the shape of a goose. However, it may not be possible to find a similar card, in which case embroider the goose on a piece of contrasting fabric and mount in a card with a standard aperture.

Materials

- Purchased blank greetings card
- Piece of cotton fabric
- White embroidery thread (coton à broder was used in this case)
- Yellow and black embroidery threads

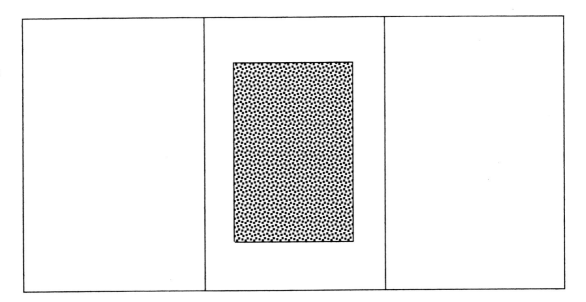

Fig.37
Lay the embroidery face down over the aperture. Secure it in place and fold the card facing over the embroidery; glue in place.

METHOD

1 Trace around the shape of the goose and transfer to a piece of cotton fabric. It will probably be necessary to work the embroidery mounted in a small hoop.

2 Embroider the goose in long and short stitch so that the stitches curve around the body and give the appearance of feathers. Try not to achieve too tidy an appearance! Embroider the beak and feet in straight stitches in yellow thread and work a french knot (see Figure 27 on page 33) for the eye.

3 Remove the embroidery from the hoop, press lightly and mount in the card. Hold the work in place with sellotape or PVA adhesive.

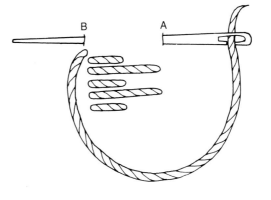

Fig.38
Long and short stitch. *This is a traditional stitch often used for shading flowers. On the first row, a long and then a short stitch are worked alternately. On all the other rows only long stitches are worked and these are fitted into the spaces made on the previous row, merging all the stitches together. To work the stitch, take the needle through the ground fabric at A and bring out again at B, close to the previous stitch.*

The goose is embroidered in long and short stitch; straight stitches are used for the beak and feet and a french knot is worked for the eye.

41

ROSES

The inspiration for the two projects here came from a 1920s embroidery magazine which featured a pretty rose design.

TABLECLOTH

This small tablecloth is worked in a form of embroidery called shadow work, and it would be suitable for a circular table, perhaps for a bedroom, conservatory or for sunny afternoons in the garden.

Shadow work was popular in the 1920s when it was used for table linen and dressing tablecloths and it was almost invariably worked on fine white fabric with matching white thread. The technique has been updated for use in the modern home and is worked on fabric that can be purchased easily today. White fabric and white thread have been chosen because they seem to suit the design perfectly. However, the cloth could be made in almost any colour, although in general the thread should always match the colour of the fabric.

Materials

- 2 m (2 yd) white polyester voile, 150 cm (60 in) wide
- 50 cm (½ yd) fusible adhesive webbing
- White embroidery thread such as coton à broder (five skeins were used for this cloth)

METHOD

1 Cut two pieces of voile, 92 cm (36 in) square. Place one of the squares to one side; this will be used later to cover the applied shapes.

2 Carefully iron the remaining strip of voile to the fusible adhesive webbing, but do not, at this stage, remove the backing paper.

3 Lay the bonded strip, paper side up, over the rose diagram (see Figure 39). Using a sharp, fine pencil, carefully trace off the design eighteen times. Reverse the pattern so that it is facing in the opposite direction and trace off eighteen more flowers.

*(Right)
The same delicate rose pattern design is used for both the bolster cushion and tablecloth.*

*Fig.39
Rose pattern. Trace off the design remembering to reverse the pattern as instructed.*

42

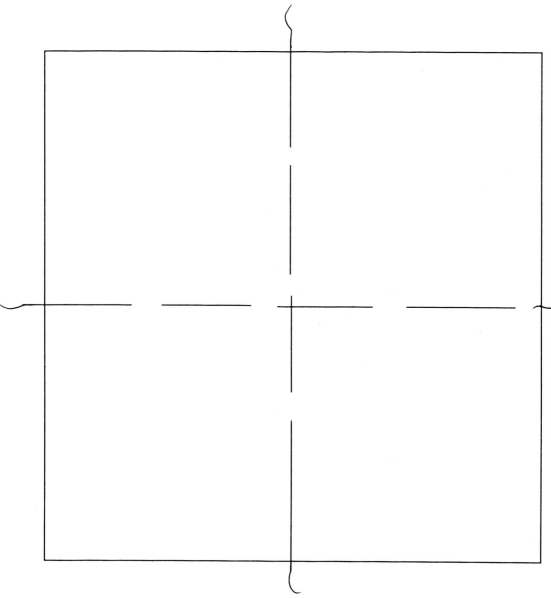

(Right)
Detail showing the corner of the tablecloth. Back stitch is used to embellish the flower heads. The embroidery is worked through all the layers of fabric.

Fig.40 (left)
Fold one square of voile into quarters and mark the quarter lines with a row of tacking stitches.

Fig.41
The flowers are arranged in a row as shown around the edge of the tablecloth.

4 Fold the square of voile into quarters and mark the quarter lines with a row of tacking stitches (see Figure 40).

5 Lay the square of voile flat on a table. The next stage is rather finicky and time consuming but it is worth taking the time to place each flower petal carefully in place.

6 The flowers are arranged in a row, facing in alternate directions (see Figure 41), around each edge of the cloth approximately 9 cm (3½ in) from the edge. Cut out each flower in turn, petal by petal, and peel off the backing paper. Arrange the petals, sticky side down, and pin each one to the backing fabric.

7 When all four borders have been laid in position, place a piece of silicone lining paper under the voile. Place another piece on top to protect the ironing board and sole plate of your iron. Carefully iron all the petals in place. Remove the pins but make sure that all the petals have been securely anchored.

8 Now trace off and cut out four more flowers for the centre of the tablecloth. Arrange them so that they lie in alternate directions, as shown in Figure 42.

9 Carefully lay the second square of voile over the top, and tack in place.

10 Using a coton à broder, or similar thread, back stitch (see Figure 18 on page 26) around each petal, through both layers of fabric.

11 When all the stitching has been worked remove the tacking threads and turn under a 2 cm (¾ in) hem.

*Fig.42
Design for the centre
of the tablecloth.*

*Detail showing the
centre of the
tablecloth.*

BOLSTER CUSHION

The same design is used for a bolster cushion, but this time it is worked in machine appliqué. A patterned floral fabric is used for the flowers and applied to a plain silk. This design would look equally successful worked in reverse, using plain flowers on a patterned fabric. Strips of the floral fabric are used as contrasting bands and piping.

Materials

- 50 cm (½ yd) cream fabric (silk noil is used for this cushion)
- 50 cm (½ yd) fine floral printed cotton
- 50 cm (½ yd) fusible adhesive webbing
- Machine sewing thread to match cream fabric
- Bolster cushion pad
- Piping cord
- Zip fastener

METHOD

1 Cut two strips of cream fabric 11 × 59 cm (4½ × 23 in). Check this measurement with your bolster cushion pad before cutting out the strips.

2 Lay the bonded strip, paper side up, over the rose pattern (see Figure 39 on page 42). Using a sharp, fine pencil, carefully trace off the design twelve times.

3 Lay the bonded paper on the reverse side of the floral fabric and press with a hot iron. Carefully cut out each rose. It is probably easier to do this one flower at a time, because so many small pieces are involved.

4 Arrange each flower in place along the length of the cream fabric strips, leaving an equal space between each flower. The flowers should all face in the same direction. Lay a sheet of silicone paper over the fabric and press well, checking that all the pieces are glued to the backing fabric.

Machine appliqué was used to create the design on this bolster cushion.

5 The petals are stitched in place with a machine zig-zag stitch. Set the zig-zag to almost the full width and the length to about 1. It will be necessary to practise first on a spare piece of fabric to obtain the correct stitch setting. Use a thread to match the cream fabric, and machine carefully around each petal.

6 Cut four strips of floral fabric 5 cm (2 in) wide and the length of the cream fabric strips, and three strips of cream fabric 2.5 cm (1 in) wide and the same length.

7 Seam all the strips together, leaving a 5 mm (¼ in) seam allowance.

It is advisable to check all these measurements against your bolster cushion pad and adjust if necessary.

8 Cut two circles of cream fabric the diameter of the cushion ends. Make a covered piping cord if required. (See General Instructions on page 18 for directions.)

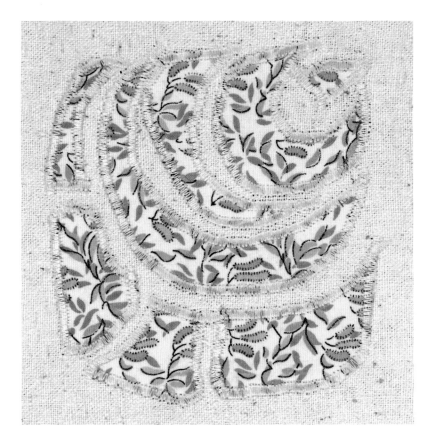

The flower pieces are stitched in place using machine zig-zag stitch.

Piping cord in matching floral fabric adds a finishing touch to the cushion.

*Fig.43
Arrange the flowers along the length of each cream strip.*

Fig.44
Seam the floral and cream strips together.

9 Insert the zip fastener in the centre of the cushion seam.
10 Pin and then tack the floral piping cord in place.
11 Carefully pin, tack and sew the fabric circles into each end of the cushion.

For extra decoration, you could attach a long tassel to each end of the completed bolster cushion. (See General Instructions, page 23, for instructions on making tassels.)

Pick out one of the colours in the contrast floral fabric.

HYDRANGEAS

A dried hydrangea arrangement is the inspiration behind these two projects. In both, hydrangea petals are used to create the embroidery designs.

MIRROR FRAME

Repeating patterns are excellent and beautiful embroidered borders can be easily worked up to surround a special mirror. A standard size self adhesive mirror tile was used here, but the design could be adapted to fit any size mirror.

METHOD

1 Cut a piece of fusible adhesive webbing, the same size as the backing fabric. Lay the tacky side of the fusible adhesive webbing on the wrong side of the fabric. Press with a hot iron until

Materials

- Self adhesive mirror tile, 22 × 22 cm (8¾ × 8¾ in)
- Backing fabric approximately 45 × 45 cm (18 × 18 in)
- Fusible adhesive webbing
- Calico approximately 45 × 45 cm (18 × 18 in)
- Scraps of sheer fabric such as organza (blues, greens and purple)
- Two or three shades of embroidery threads to match
- Backing board
- Strong string
- PVA adhesive

A repeating hydrangea border design using blue, green and purple organzas is adapted for this mirror frame. The embroidery is worked over the petals in matching threads.

both pieces are firmly glued together. Peel off the paper backing fabric and lay the fabric, sticky side down, on to a piece of calico. Press both fabrics firmly together.

2 Place the fabric on a flat surface and mark the centres with a row of horizontal and vertical tacking stitches (see Figure 45). Carefully mark a square 22 × 22 cm (9¾ × 9¾ in) in the centre of the fabric. It is a good idea to mark this shape with tacking threads.

3 Iron the scraps of sheer fabric to scraps of fusible adhesive webbing but do not at this stage remove the paper backing. Trace the outlines of the three larger hydrangea flowers (see Figure 46) onto the paper backing.

4 Carefully cut out each flower, peel off the paper backing and lay them on the backing fabric. Use the illustration as a guide, but arrange them to your own satisfaction, overlapping the flowers as you work. When the border has been completed, lay a piece of silicone paper over the shapes to avoid a residue of adhesive on the iron sole plate and press them firmly in place.

5 If required, mount the fabric on a square frame to work the embroidery. (See General Instructions on page 10.)

6 Embroider the outline of each petal in back stitch (see Figure 18 on page 26). Do not follow the outlines of each petal exactly, but in places take the stitches over the edges of the applied

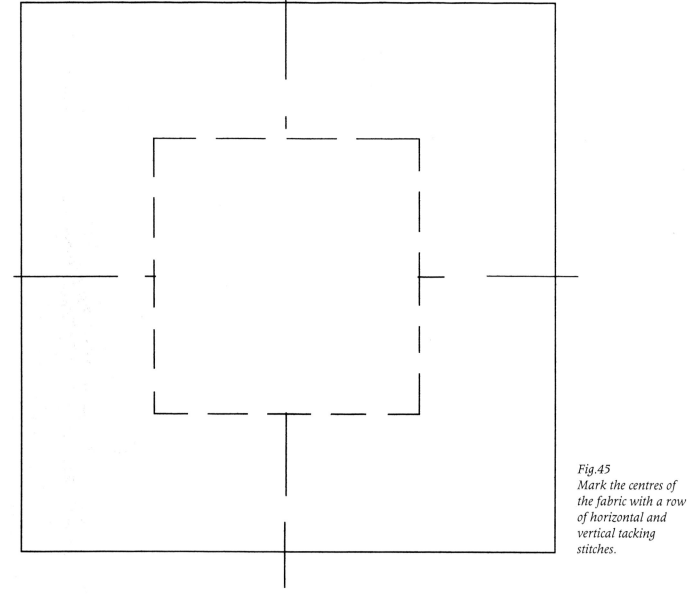

Fig.45
Mark the centres of the fabric with a row of horizontal and vertical tacking stitches.

fabrics. Vary the colour of the thread in each flower. Using Figure 47 as a guide, stitch the lines inside the petals in running stitch (see Figure 22 on page 29), and the centres in tiny back stitches, worked in pairs in any direction. This stitch is often called dot stitch (see Figure 46). Again, referring to Figure 47 as a guide, use a soft pencil and lightly draw the smaller flowers onto the fabric, embroidering them as described for the larger flowers.

7 When all the embroidery has been worked, remove the fabric from the frame. If a frame has not been used it may be necessary to dampen and

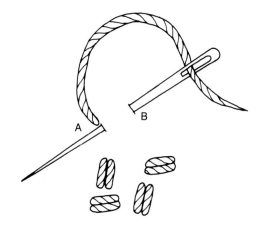

Fig.46
Dot stitch. *This is a similar stitch to seeding and is really just two tiny stitches worked in pairs. Bring the needle out of the fabric at A and return it to B.*

The outline of each petal is embroidered in simple back stitch and the lines inside the petals are embroidered in running stitch. Tiny back stitches, worked in pairs, are used in the centres of the flowers.

Fig.47
Trace the outlines of the three larger hydrangea flowers on to the paper backing of the bonded fabrics.

Fig.48
Place the mirror tile in the centre of the piece of card, then take one of the pieces of card with an aperture and glue in place around the mirror.

stretch the work slightly (see General Instruction, page 16).

8 Cut three pieces of strong card, 34.5 × 34.5 cm (13½ × 13½ in). Cut a central aperture, 22 × 22 cm (8¾ × 8¾ in), in two of the pieces. (If you are not used to cutting card mounts, you may prefer to have them cut by a professional picture framer.)

9 Place the mirror tile in the centre of the card without an aperture and glue it in place. Take one of the pieces of card with an aperture and glue it in place around the mirror. Leave to dry.

10 To mount the embroidery, lay the fabric right side up on a flat surface. Carefully cut away the fabric about 2 cm (¾ in) inside the tacked square. Then, using sharp pointed scissors, snip very carefully into the corners, up to the tacking stitches.

11 Turn the fabric to the wrong side and lay the third piece of card on top carefully matching up the corners. Use pins to hold the card and fabric in place. Take out all the tacking stitches.

12 Spread a thin layer of adhesive around the edges of the card aperture. Pull the fabric carefully over the card frame to the wrong side, a small section at a time, and finger press in place. Leave to dry thoroughly.

13 When the adhesive is dry place the embroidered mount over the mirror. Turn to the back and lace the fabric over all the pieces of card and finish as described in General Instructions (see page 18).

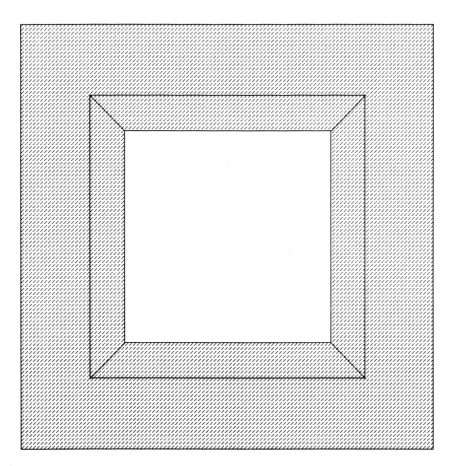

Fig.49
Lay the embroidery right side up on a flat surface and carefully cut away the fabric about 2 cm (¾ in) inside the tacked square. Snip carefully into the corners up to the tacking stitches.

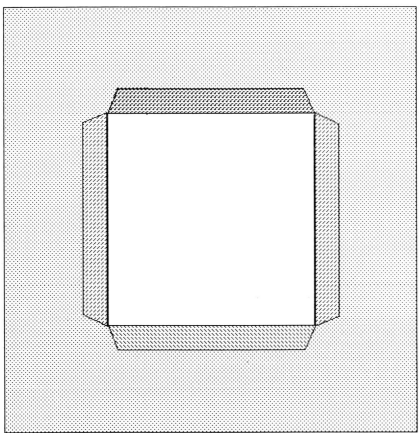

Fig.50
Lay the third piece of card over the wrong side of the embroidery. Spread adhesive around the edges of the card aperture and pull the fabric through, glueing it to the card frame on the wrong side.

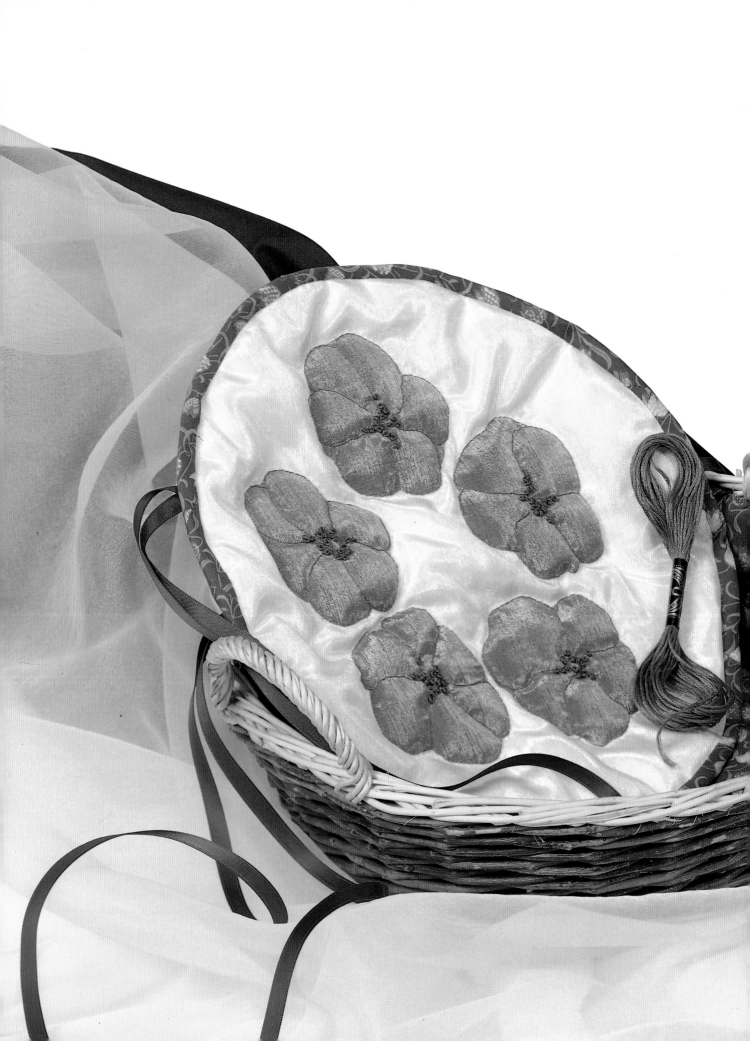

WORKBASKET

Hydrangea petals were used as inspiration to create this basket lid worked in shadow quilting. A matching printed cotton was chosen for the basket lining.

The basket used here has a diameter of 26.5 cm (10½ in), but you may need to adapt the design to fit the dimensions of your own basket as sizes vary so much. Select brightly coloured fabric for the applied flowers, as they will become quite subdued when covered with a piece of transparent fabric.

METHOD

1 For the lid measure the diameter of the top of the basket. Add 1.5 cm (½ in) for the turning and draw a paper pattern circle to this size. Lay the pattern on the white cotton fabric and lightly outline the shape using an HB or H pencil. Do not cut out the circle.

Materials
- Brightly coloured fabric for applied flowers, 25 × 25 cm (9¾ × 9¾ in)
- Fusible adhesive webbing
- White crystal nylon organza, or other transparent fabric, approximately 33 × 33 cm (13 × 13 in)
- Piece of white cotton fabric or similar, approximately 33 × 33 cm (13 × 13 in)
- Square of butter muslin, approximately 33 × 33 cm (13 × 13 in)
- Skein of embroidery thread to match colour of hydrangea flowers
- 50 cm (½ yd) of 2 oz terylene wadding
- 1 m (1 yd) of cotton fabric for lining basket and lid
- Matching narrow ribbon

2 Trace five outlines of the large hydrangea onto the fusible adhesive webbing. Iron the brightly coloured fabric to the fusible adhesive webbing as described for the mirror frame (see page 51) and cut out each petal.

3 Peel off the backing paper and arrange the flowers, adhesive side down, round the centre of the white fabric. Place a piece of silicone paper over the flowers and iron them in place.

4 Lay the butter muslin on a flat surface and lay a square of wadding over it. Place the fabric with the flower shapes on top of the wadding and finally the square of crystal nylon organza. Tack all the layers together.

Refer to the section on Quilting (see page 28) for more detailed information on preparing fabrics for quilting.

5 For the quilting, outline all the flowers in back stitch (see Figure 18 on page 26). Work french knots (see Figure 27 on page 33) in the centre of each flower.

6 When all the embroidery has been worked, lay the paper circle pattern on the top of the quilted fabric and redraw

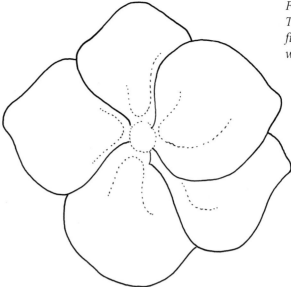

Fig.51
Trace the outline on to fusible adhesive webbing.

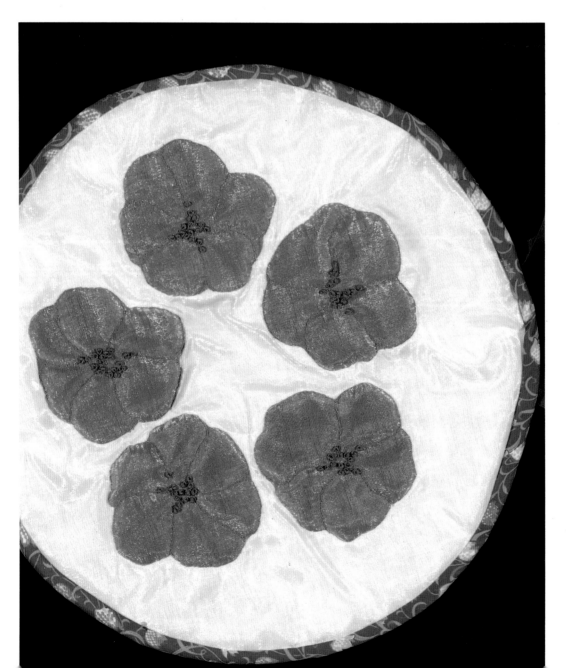

The petals are outlined in back stitch and french knots are worked into the centre of each flower.

The workbasket interior is lined with matching cotton fabric.

the outline if necessary. Cut away the excess fabric.

7 For the lid lining, using the paper circle as a pattern, cut a circle from the cotton lining fabric and place it, right side up, over the butter muslin. Pin or tack the layers together.

8 Cut a length of bias fabric from the lining fabric (see instructions on page 19). Pin one edge of the bias strip, right sides together, to the top of the lid. Pin, tack and machine in place. Trim the raw edges; turn the bias strip to the other side and hem stitch in place.

9 If the basket has handles, cut strips of matching narrow ribbon for ties, fold them in half and stitch to the underside of the lid.

Lining the basket

1 Measure the circumference of the basket. Measure the depth of the basket and add 2 cm (¾ in) to each of these measurements.

2 Cut a strip of lining fabric, one and a half times the measurement of the circumference of the basket and twice the measurement of the depth of the basket.

3 Machine the narrow ends together to make one long continuous strip.

4 Press the strip in half, with the wrong sides together.

5 Using a strong thread such as linen or buttonhole thread, stitch the lining to the basket, just beneath the rim, gathering the fabric evenly as you work.

6 Measure the diameter of the base of the basket and cut a circle in thin card to this measurement.

7 Place the card on the lining fabric and cut out a fabric circle, including turnings of at least 2 cm (¾ in). Cut a circle of wadding, the same size as the card circle.

8 Run a gathering thread around the edge of the fabric. Place the wadding over the card and place the fabric, right side up, over the wadding.

9 Draw up the gathering thread so that the turnings are drawn over the card and place the fabric-covered card in the base of the basket. If the measurements are correct, it will not be necessary to glue the base in place.

$\mathscr{L}$AVENDER

Flowers and herbs have always been favourite inspirations for embroiderers and lavender has been selected for the photograph frame, panel and bag in this section.

PHOTOGRAPH FRAME

When choosing embroidery threads for these projects, it is important to match the colour of the thread to the colour of lavender. Flower threads, which are fine matt cotton threads, seemed especially appropriate.

Materials

- Backing fabric, approximately 29 × 24 cm (11½ × 9½ in) (the fabric used here is a natural coloured slubbed silk)
- Calico, approximately 29 × 24 cm (11½ × 9½ in)
- Fusible adhesive webbing
- Embroidery threads in shades of green and lavender
- Card for mount and backing
- Strong string
- PVA adhesive

METHOD

1 Cut a piece of fusible adhesive webbing the same size as the backing fabric. Lay the tacky side of the webbing on the wrong side of the fabric. Press with a hot iron until both pieces are firmly glued together. Peel off the paper backing and lay the fabric, sticky side down, on to a piece of calico. Press both fabrics firmly together.

2 Mark the centre of the fabric with a line of vertical and horizontal tacking stitches. Then, mark a rectangle, 9 × 14 cm (3½ × 5½ in) in the centre of the fabric with tacking stitches.

3 Trace off the lavender stems and transfer them to the fabric (see General Instructions on page 13). On the photograph frame illustrated, I have placed one flower on the left hand side and two overlapping flowers on the right, but you may wish to vary this arrangement. Mount the fabric in a hoop to work the embroidery.

4 Work the flower stems first in stem stitch (Figure 54) and the leaves in satin stitch (see Figure 19 on page 26). Embroider the flowers in detached chain stitch (see Figure 55) working the stitches in pairs, on either side of the stem. To complete the embroidery scatter single detached chain stitches around the flowers.

5 When the embroidery has been worked, remove the fabric from the hoop and press the wrong side lightly with a warm iron.

6 Cut two pieces of card, each 23 × 18 cm (9 × 7¼ in). Cut an aperture 9 × 14 cm (3½ × 5½ in) in the centre of one of the pieces.

7 Lay the fabric right side up on a flat surface. Carefully cut away the fabric about 2 cm (¾ in) inside the tacked oblong. Then, using sharp pointed scissors snip very carefully into the corners of the oblong.

8 Turn the fabric to the wrong side and lay the card with the aperture over the embroidery, carefully matching up the corners. It is a good idea to use pins to hold the fabric and card together at this stage. Remove all the tacking threads.

9 Spread a thin layer of PVA adhesive around the edges of the card aperture. Pull the fabric carefully over the card frame, a small section at a time, and press in place with your fingers. Leave to dry thoroughly.

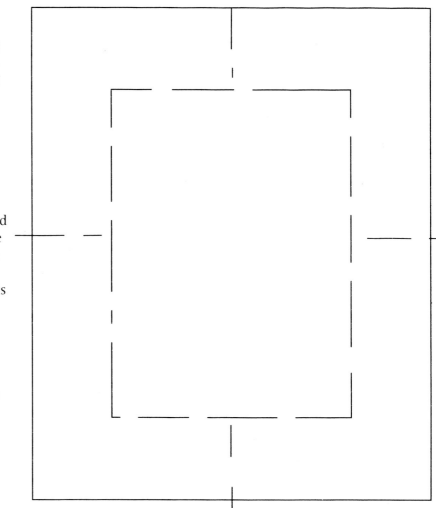

Fig.52 (above)
Mark the centre of the fabric with tacking lines.

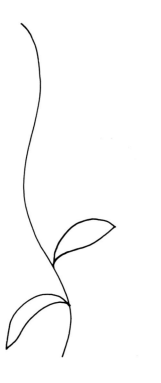

Fig.53 (left)
Trace off the lavender stems and transfer them to the fabric.

10 Centre the photograph over the backing card; glue in place and leave until completely dry.

11 Lay the embroidered mount over the backing card, take the edges to the wrong side and lace together (see General Instructions on page 18).

12 Cut a piece of calico (or fabric to match the front of the frame, if preferred) slightly larger than the card. Turn under and press the raw edges; lay the fabric over the back of the frame and hem stitch in place.

13 If the photograph frame is to be hung on the wall, finish as in General Instructions on page 17. If it is to stand, cut a strip of card 12 × 4 cm (4¾ × 1¼ in) and glue firmly to the back of the card.

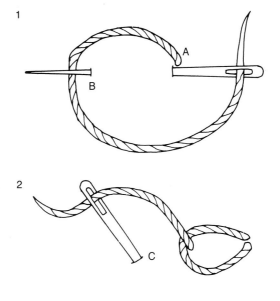

Fig.55
Detached chain stitch or lazy daisy stitch. *1. Bring the needle out of the fabric at A. Re-insert it at the same point and then bring out again at B, with the thread lying under the needle. 2. Re-insert the needle at C to complete the stitch.*

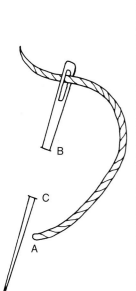

Fig.54
Stem stitch. *Always keep the thread to the right of the needle. Bring the needle through the fabric at A and insert it at B. Bring it out again at C ready to work the next stitch.*

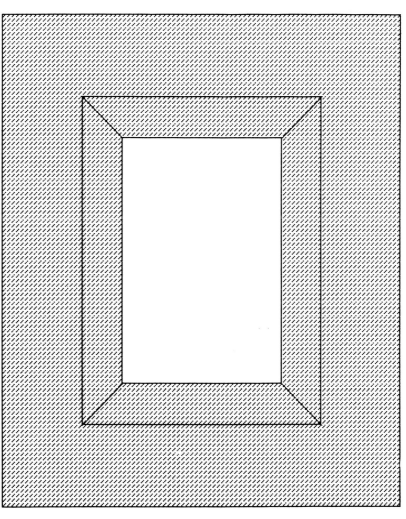

Fig.56
Carefully cut away the centre of the embroidered fabric and snip into the corners of the oblong.

(Left)
Lavender and green embroidery threads and simple stitches are used to decorate the pretty silk frame. This design is repeated on the small lavender bag and the panel on page 66.

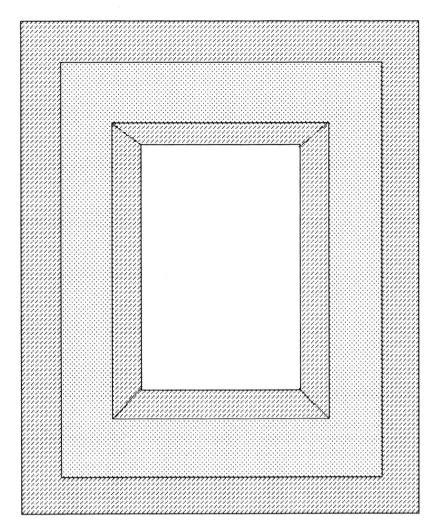

Fig.57
Lay the card with the aperture over the embroidery, matching the corners. Spread adhesive around the aperture edges and pull the fabric carefully over the card frame. Finger press in place and leave to dry.

(Below)
This small bag is filled with dried lavender. The flower is worked in stem stitch and satin stitch and the tiny lavender petals are embroiderd in detached chain stitch.

LAVENDER BAG

The lavender bag was made quickly and simply from scraps of calico.

1 Cut two pieces of calico, approximately 11 × 9 cm (4½ × 3½ in).
2 Embroider a lavender flower, as described on page 61, on one piece of calico.
3 Place the two pieces, wrong sides together, and machine around three sides, approximately 1.5 cm (½ in) from the edge. Fill the sachet with dried lavender and close the fourth side with a row of machining. Trim the raw edges with pinking shears and stitch a row of lace around the edges.

PANEL

The lavender flowers have been used this time as a repeating pattern on a small picture. The embroidery is worked on a background of calico, using fine silk threads, and has been mounted in a purchased card mount and frame. The design would look equally effective as a panel in the centre of a cushion.

Materials

- Calico, approximately 35 × 30 cm (14 × 12 in)
- Fine silk embroidery threads in 'lavender' colours
- Card mount to fit purchased frame
- A piece of backing board the same size as the frame

METHOD

1 Mark the centre of the calico with rows of tacking stitches.
2 Trace the design onto tracing or greaseproof paper and transfer to the fabric (see General Instructions on page 13). The stems and leaves on the

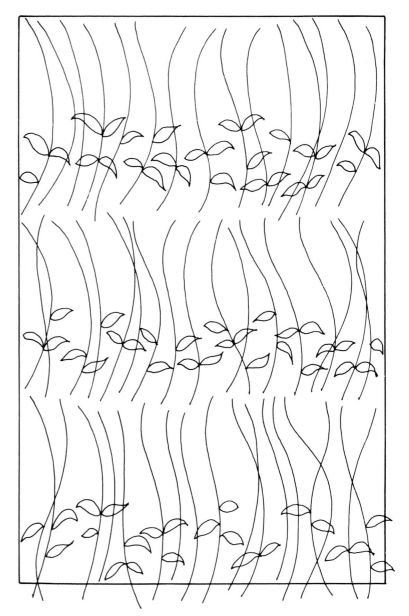

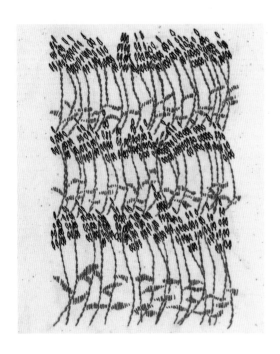

diagram are guides; add extra stems and leaves as you work the embroidery. Mount the fabric in a small frame or embroidery hoop.
3 Work the embroidery as described for the photograph frame on page 61.
4 When the embroidery has been completed, take it out of the frame or hoop. Remove all the tacking threads and press lightly on the wrong side.
5 Cut a piece of backing fabric the same size as the card mount and make up the panel as described in General Instructions (see page 17).

Fig.58 (above)
Trace off the design and transfer it to the fabric.

(Left and right)
Rows of lavender create a simple design for a small panel. This picture can be worked fairly quickly using fine matt cotton embroidery threads.

$\mathcal{K}$NOT GARDENS

*These formal geometrical gardens were popular
in Elizabethan times and were often planted
with sweet smelling herbs, such as lavender
or thyme.*

HERB PILLOW

The design for this small herb pillow
was taken from an early English knot
garden. The embroidery is worked in a
technique called Italian quilting, with
some added hand stitches. White silk
was used to make the cushion, but any
fine silky fabric would be appropriate.

METHOD

1 Mark the centre of one of the silk
squares with lines of tacking stitches
(see Figure 59).
2 Transfer the design to the fabric using
the tracing and tacking method (see
General Instructions on page 13), taking
care to match the centres of the design
to the tacked lines on the fabric (see
Figures 60 and 61).

3 Pin the square of butter muslin to the
wrong side of the fabric and tack the
two layers together.
4 Stitch around all the outlines of the
design, using small running stitches (see
Figure 22 on page 29), or back stitch
(see Figure 18 on page 26) if you prefer.
5 Thread a large, blunt-eyed needle
with a length of quilting wool. Working
from the wrong side of the fabric, take
the quilting wool through the butter
muslin only, and thread it through all
the stitched channels (see Figure 59).
Leave a loop of wool at each corner of
the design to prevent the work from
puckering. In this design the channels

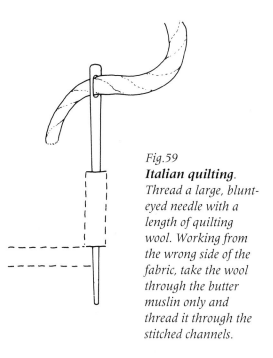

Fig.59
Italian quilting*.
Thread a large, blunt-
eyed needle with a
length of quilting
wool. Working from
the wrong side of the
fabric, take the wool
through the butter
muslin only and
thread it through the
stitched channels.*

*(Left)
White silk and
matching embroidery
threads are used for
the small herb pillow
which is filled with
sweet smelling pot
pourri.*

Materials

- Two pieces of white silk fabric,
approximately 27 × 27 cm (10½ ×
10½ in)
- Butter muslin, 27 × 27 cm (10½ ×
10½ in)
- Quilting wool
- Embroidery thread in colour to
match the cushion fabric (fine cotton
perlé was used)
- 2 oz terylene wadding
- Pot pourri

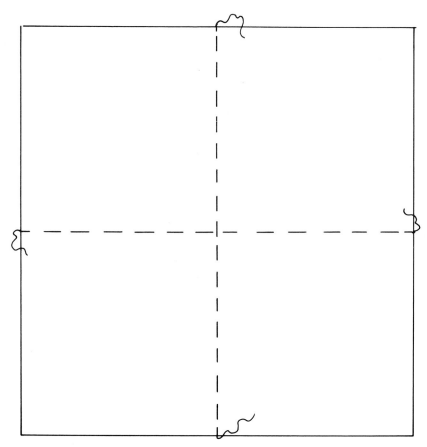

cross each other, so it will be necessary to slip the quilting wool underneath the first row at the intersections.

6 When the quilting has been completed, turn the work to the right side and complete the design with simple embroidery stitches. French knots (see Figure 27 on page 33) are worked in the spaces inside the knot garden, and seeding stitches (see Figure 20 on page 26) are worked over the rest of the fabric. White threads are used here but coloured threads could be used, if desired.

7 To make up the pillow, place the two pieces of silk right sides together and machine stitch around three sides. Insert the cushion filling and slip stitch the opening. As it was not possible to buy a standard cushion pad for such a small cushion, a length of terylene wadding was folded to the correct size and inserted. Pot pourri was placed inside the folds.

Fig.60
Mark the centre of one of the silk squares with horizontal and vertical lines of tacking stitches.

The central pattern of the cushion is worked in Italian quilting. The design is completed with simple embroidery stitches. French knots are worked in the spaces and seeding stitches are worked over the rest of the fabric.

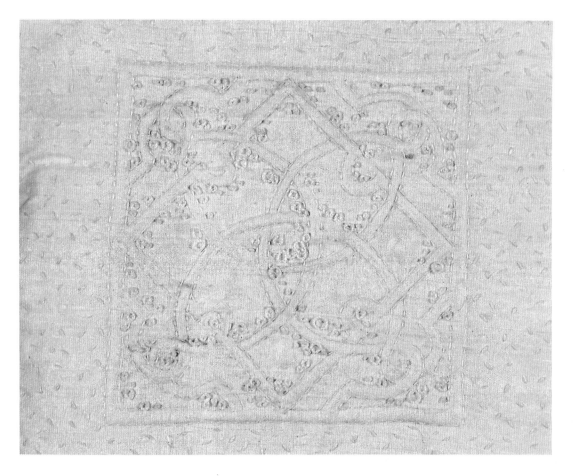

Fig.61
Trace the design on to greaseproof or tracing paper.

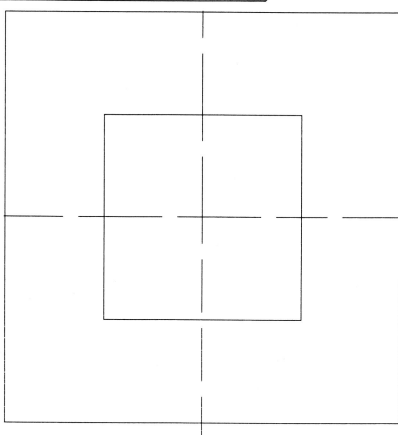

Fig.62
Transfer the design to the fabric, taking care to match the centres of the design to the tacked lines on the fabric.

PINCUSHION

A simpler knot garden design was used for the pincushion, which is worked in shadow quilting.

Materials

- Small piece of sheer fabric, such as crystal nylon
- Dark cotton fabric, 30 × 30 cm (12 ×12 in)
- Pieces of brightly coloured felt
- Matching embroidery thread

METHOD

1 Cut a piece of dark cotton backing fabric, approximately 14 cm (5½ in) square.

2 Using greaseproof or tracing paper, trace off the design of the smaller knot garden (see Figure 63) and cut out the shapes in felt. Choose brightly coloured felts as the colours will be very subdued when covered with crystal nylon. Lay them on the backing fabric in the design of the knot garden.

3 Cut a square of sheer fabric, the same size as the backing and lay it carefully over the embroidery, taking care not to move the felt shapes. (These could be tacked down first if you prefer.) Pin or tack all the layers together.

4 Using a fine embroidery thread, and working through both layers of fabric, outline all the felt shapes in back stitch (see Figure 18 on page 26). Further embroidery stitches could be added at this stage if you wish.

5 Cut a square of backing fabric, the same size as the other squares, and make up in the same way as the herb pillow. Bran is a useful filling for pincushions, as it absorbs moisture. Finish by stitching a simple, twisted hand made cord around the edges (see General Instructions on page 21).

(Left)
Coloured felts, crystal nylon and matching embroidery threads are used to create this knot garden design.

Fig.63
Trace off the design and cut out the shapes in brightly coloured felt.

WALLHANGING

This elaborate design is in cream silk fabric with some added surface embroidery stitches. The quilting is worked by hand, using a fine white sewing silk. The following instructions are for a slightly simpler version of the wall hanging shown here and would be equally suitable for a small cot quilt or pram quilt. A good-quality polyester cotton or a pure cotton with a slight sheen could be substituted for the silk.

METHOD

The large knot garden (Figure 64) is repeated four times in the centre of the wallhanging and the smaller knot garden (Figure 65) makes up the border. You will find it easier to trace

Materials

- 1 × 1 m (1 × 1 yd) cream or white silk
- 1 m (1 yd) 20 oz terylene wadding
- 1 m (1 yd) butter muslin or fine cotton for backing
- Fine cream or white sewing silk (or 1 reel cream or white quilting thread)
- 1 skein cream or white stranded embroidery thread
- Quilting needle
- Black felt-tip waterproof pen
- Fine pencil
- Large sheet of tracing paper, approx. 75 × 75 cm (30 × 30 in) (it may be necessary to tape several smaller sheets together)
- Masking tape

Fig. 64
The design for the large knot garden.

the whole design on to tracing paper and then transfer it to the fabric.

1 Fold the sheet of tracing paper in half and into quarters to find the centre lines. Lay the tracing paper over Figure 64, so that it lies approximately 2 cm (¾ in) out from the centre foldlines. Using a black waterproof pen, carefully trace off all the lines. Repeat this three times, spacing the blocks at equal distance from the centre foldlines.

2 Use a ruler to draw a line around the four blocks 2 cm (¾ in) away, following the dotted lines in Figure 66. Draw a second line 2 cm (¾ in) from the first. Refer to Figure 66 for the layout.

3 Lay the sheet of tracing paper over the smaller knot garden (Figure 65) so that it lies in the centre of the folded line and approximately 2 cm (¾ in) above the outer ruled line. Trace it twice on either side of the large centre knot garden, spacing the gardens equally apart. Repeat this on the other three sides of the tracing paper, referring to Figure 66 for the layout.

4 Use a ruler to draw a line around the outside edge of the blocks 2 cm (¾ in) away, following the dotted lines on Figure 66. Draw a second line 2 cm (¾ in) from the first, then a third line the same distance away.

5 Before transferring the design to fabric, cut a strip of white silk approximately 30 cm (8 in) along the length of the fabric, to bind the edges of the hanging.

6 Lay the tracing paper on a flat surface and tape firmly in place with masking tape.

7 Place the white silk over the tracing paper, taking care to match the centres. It is a good idea to tape the fabric in place as it will take some time to transfer the design. Using a fine pencil, transfer the design to the fabric (see General Instructions, page 13).

8 Cut a piece of butter muslin and wadding, both slightly larger than the top fabric. Place the muslin on a flat

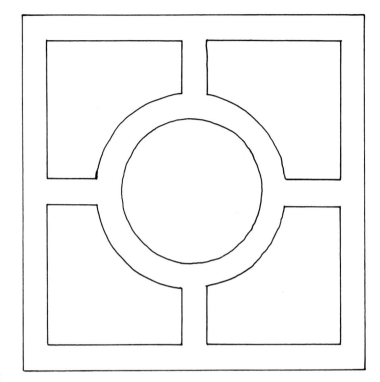

Fig. 65
The smaller knot garden forms the outer border of the design.

surface and cover with the wadding. Place the top fabric over the wadding and smooth in place. Tack all three layers together. Refer to the section on Quilting (page 28) for more detailed instructions.

9 Starting from the centre of the design and using running stitches (see Figure 22 on page 29), quilt all the lines marked on the fabric. Trim away the excess fabric but leave an unquilted strip approximately 2.5 cm (1 in) beyond this line to form a border.

10 To finish, embroider french knots (see Figure 27 on page 33) around the circles in each of the small knot gardens.

11 Cut four strips of silk 4 cm (1½ in) wide and the length of each side.

12 With right sides together, pin and tack one of the strips to one edge of the hanging. Machine stitch in place. Repeat with the other three sides.

13 Turn each strip to the wrong side, turn under the raw edges and hem neatly in place.

14 If the work is to be a wallhanging, cut a strip of calico the width of the quilt and 13 cm (5 in) wide. Fold the

strip in half lengthways and machine
the long edges together. Turn the strip
to the right side and press. Turn under
the raw edges and slipstitch them
together.

15 Decide which is to be the top edge
of the wallhanging and pin the calico
strip to this edge, on the wrong side.
Hem both long sides to the back of the
hanging, leaving the shorter sides open.
Slip a length of dowel inside the casing.

Fig. 66
*The layout of the
wallhanging. The
large knot garden is
repeated four times in
the centre. The small
squares represent the
smaller knot garden.
The dotted lines
indicate rows of
quilting stitches.*

$\mathcal{P}$OPPIES

Poppies are used as a source of inspiration for a café curtain, a workbag and a panel, and all three projects are worked in simple machine embroidery.

MACHINE EMBROIDERY

Machine embroidery is not a difficult technique and any straight stitch sewing machine can be used for these projects. You do not need a lot of equipment, apart from a sewing machine, although a ring hoop is essential. It is possible to buy a machine embroidery hoop in specialist embroidery shops and they will also supply machine embroidery threads in a wide range of colours. Make sure that you have a plentiful supply of machine needles – sizes 90 or 100 are probably best. Scraps of fabric, such as sheeting or calico, are ideal for practising.

Although I have said that any straight stitch sewing machine can be used, do make sure that you have the machine hand book to refer to.

There are some important rules to follow when you are doing machine embroidery. These are:

1 Remove the presser foot. Some machines provide a darning foot which can be used instead.
2 Lower or cover the feed dog. Some sewing machines have a plate to cover it if it is not possible to lower it.
3 Set the stitch length to 0.
4 Place the fabric in a ring frame so that it is drum tight and sits flat on the bed of the sewing machine.
5 Place the fabric on the bed of the machine. Manually turn the fly wheel so that the needle is inserted into the fabric and the bobbin thread is brought up to the surface.
6 Lower the presser foot. It is important to remember to do this and, if you are a beginner, probably easier to remember if a darning foot is used rather than no foot at all.
7 Begin stitching, moving the framed fabric carefully and rather slowly at first. Practise 'drawing' shapes, swirls, curved lines across the fabric until you feel competent to progress further.

CAFÉ CURTAIN

Poppies are applied on to the café curtain and then machine embroidered. The flowers are worked in white on a white background fabric, but could equally well be worked in colour.

METHOD

This particular curtain was made to hang in a small window and is 84 cm

Materials

- White cotton organdie (see text for measurements)
- Matching machine embroidery thread

(Right)
A pretty white poppy design is appliquéd on to a white café curtain and machine embroidery is used to outline the pattern.

(33 in) wide and 66 cm (26 in) deep. You will need to measure your own window and adjust the fabric requirements accordingly. A café curtain is usually the width of the window, without any gathers, and covers the bottom half of the window.

Allow 4 cm (1½ in) at each side for hems. Add 11.5 cm (4½ in) to the length of the curtain for hems. An extra 15 cm (6 in) will be needed for the facing and, if the flowers are to be in the same fabric, allow extra fabric for the poppies. A white cotton organdie was chosen for the curtain as it is quite sheer and rather stiff.

1 Cut out the curtain to the measurements of the window, plus turnings for side hems, and cut a 15 cm (6 in) strip for facing.

2 Use the remaining fabric to cut out the flower shapes that are to be applied to the curtain. Using tracing paper, trace off the outline of the larger poppy (see Figure 67). Cut around the paper poppy and pin the pattern to the fabric; cut around the pattern without a turning. Repeat for as many poppies as required. Seven flowers were used for the curtain shown here, but if you are making a wider curtain you will need to cut out more flowers.

3 Lay the curtain right side up on a flat surface and arrange the flowers on the fabric. When you have achieved a satisfactory arrangement, pin and tack the flowers in place.

4 Using a soluble marker or pencil, lightly draw in the lines illustrated on the poppy in Figure 67, and draw in the stems also.

5 Thread the sewing machine with matching embroidery thread and, following the instructions in the Machine embroidery section (see page 78), stitch around the outline of each of the flowers to hold them in place. Add extra lines of stitching to bring them to life. You will find that no two flowers will look the same and this adds greatly to the charm of the embroidery. When you have stitched the flower embroider the stems in the same way, tapering off the stitching to a fine line at the base of each stem.

6 When all the embroidery has been worked, remove the tacking threads, trim any ends of threads, and press the fabric well with a steam iron.

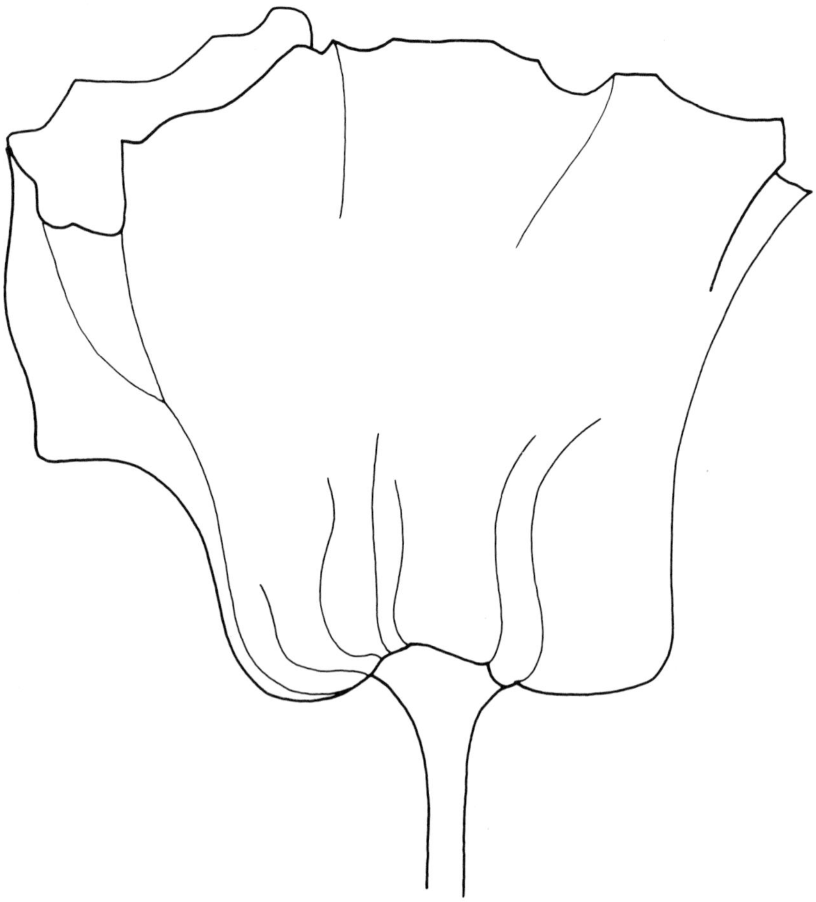

Making up the curtain

1 For the scalloped heading, trace off the template (see Figure 68) and transfer it to a piece of thin card.

2 Beginning approximately 5 cm (2 in) from one end, mark a scallop on the top of the curtain with a soft pencil. Leaving 2 cm (¾ in) between each scallop, continue marking with the template until you reach the other edge of the curtain (see Figure 69). You will probably need to adjust the turnings at each side of the curtain.

Fig.67
Trace this poppy outline and cut it out around the edge. Pin the pattern to the fabric and cut out as many flowers as you will need.

Detail of the embroidered poppy design.

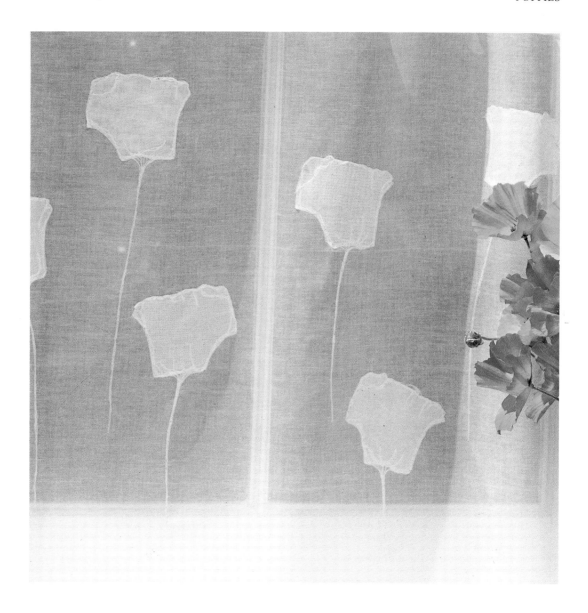

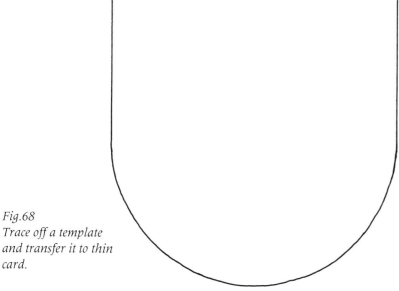

*Fig.68
Trace off a template and transfer it to thin card.*

3 Turn up a small double hem on the facing fabric and stitch in place. With right sides together pin and tack the facing to the top of the curtain.

4 Pin and tack the two fabrics together, working around the scallops and across the top of the curtain (see Figure 70). Mark a 1.5 cm (½ in) seam line at each side and across the straight edge of the curtain.

5 Carefully machine first one side of the curtain and facing, then machine around each scallop across the curtain and down the other side of the facing, pivoting the machine needle as you stitch. Remove all the tacking threads and trim away the excess fabric. Snip into the seam allowances at all the curves.

6 Turn in and slip stitch a double hem down each side of the curtain, snipping into the seam allowance at the base of the facing. Turn up and hand stitch the lower hem.

7 Carefully turn the facing right side out and press in place. Sew curtain rings to the top of the curtain between each scallop.

8 Hang the café curtain from a brass rod or wooden pole, cut to fit your window measurement.

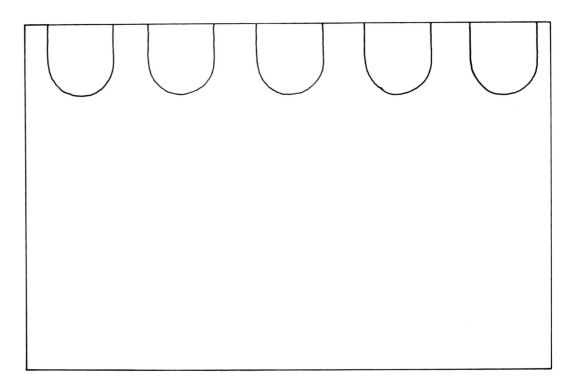

Fig.69
Beginning at on end of the curtain heading, mark a row of scallops.

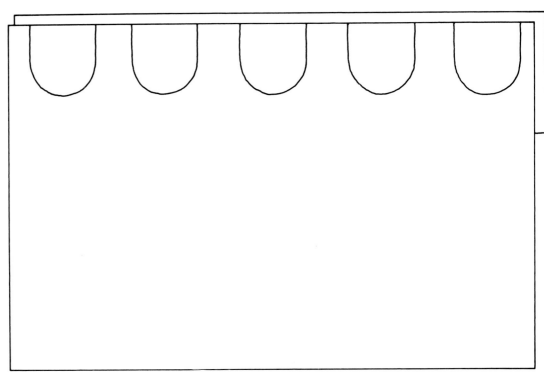

Fig.70
Pin and tack the facing and curtain together.

WORKBAG

The instructions for this double-sided workbag were among several found in embroidery magazines from the early part of this century. This bag has been made and lined in calico, but any cotton fabric or furnishing fabric would be suitable. If you use calico choose one of good quality and preferably one that has been pre-shrunk. The poppies were stencilled on the fabric and then machine embroidered.

Calico workbag with the stencilled design worked in matching threads.

Materials

- Tracing paper
- Card, or oiled stencil card
- 1 m (1 yd) calico
- Small piece of terylene wadding
- Red fabric paint
- Stencil brush or sponge
- Machine embroidery threads in red, green and dark brown
- Two lengths of cord, each 100 cm (39 in)

METHOD

1 Cut four strips of calico, each 70 × 23 cm (27½ × 9¼ in).

2 To make the stencil, use greaseproof paper or tracing paper. Trace around the outlines of the two smaller poppies (see Figure 71), and transfer each to a separate piece of card or oiled stencil card (see General Instructions on page 13). Remember to leave plenty of card around the shape of each poppy, or it will be difficult to apply the fabric paint. Using a sharp craft knife, carefully cut around the outlines of the flowers.

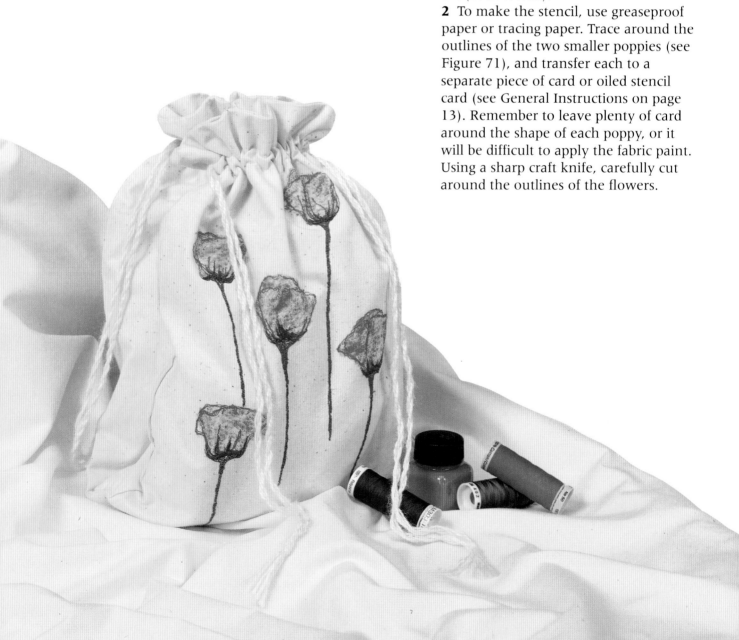

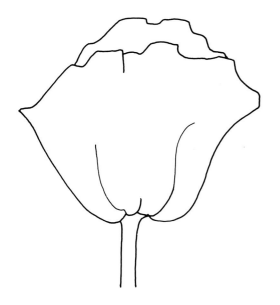

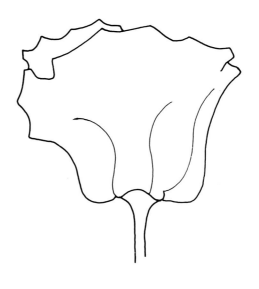

Fig.71
Trace around the outlines of the poppies and transfer each to a separate piece of card, or oiled stencil card.

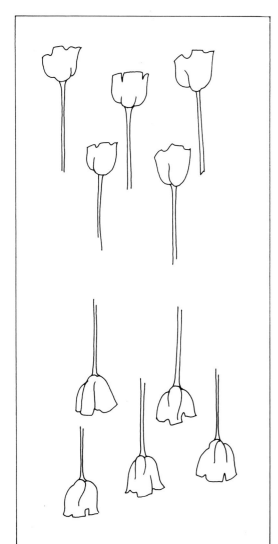

Fig.72 (far left)
Place the poppies in a similar arrangement to those shown here, reversing the design as illustrated.

Fig.73 (left)
Mark the top and bottom edges of the fabric as instructed.

*Fig. 74 (left)
With right sides together, machine one of the other strips of fabric to the embroidered strip, leaving the seam open between the marks.*

*(Below)
Detail of the stencilled poppy design.*

5 When the paint is dry, iron the back of the fabric to set it. Using a soft pencil, lightly draw in each stem.

6 Referring to the Machine embroidery section on page 78, embroider over the stencilled flowers in red machine embroidery thread, adding the petal shapes. Use dark brown thread to form the base of each flower. Work the stems in the same way in green thread, tapering each stem to a fine line at the base.

7 When all the embroidery has been worked, trim away any odd threads and press the embroidery on the wrong side.

8 Mark a point 4 cm (1½ in) from the top edge and another point 2 cm (¾ in) below. Make the same marks at the other side of the strip, and repeat at the other end of the strip of fabric.

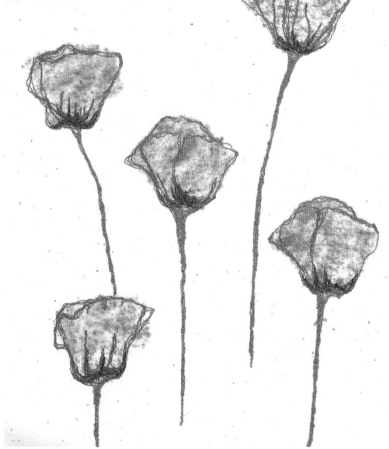

3 Lay one of the strips of calico right side up on a flat surface, and place one of the stencils over it, about 6 cm (2¾ in) from the narrow edge.

4 Using either a dry sponge or a stencil brush, lightly dab red fabric paint through the stencil. Make sure the paint is completely dry before lifting the stencil away. Place the stencil near to the first flower and repeat the procedure four times, arranging the poppies in a similar arrangement to those shown in the photograph (right). Repeat the stencils at the other end of the fabric strip, but remember to reverse the flowers, as shown in Figure 72.

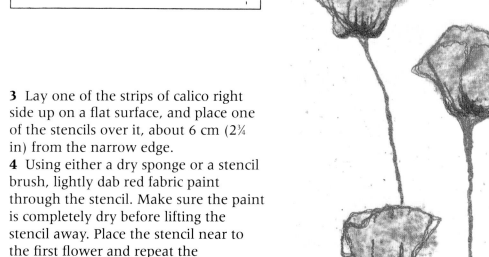

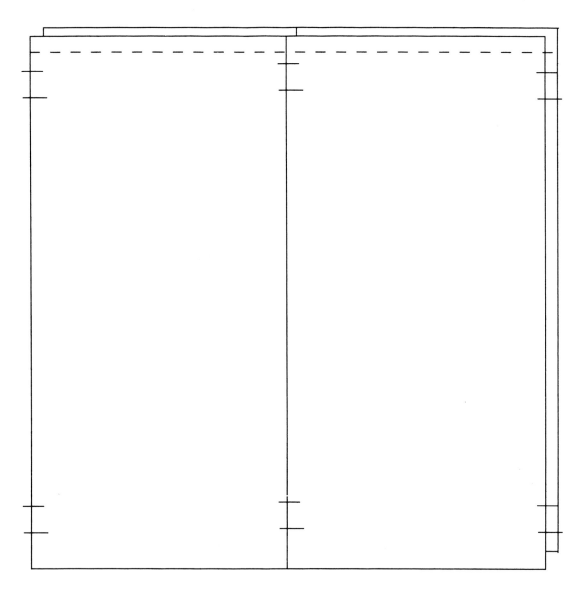

Fig.75 (left)
With right sides
facing, pin and
machine the lining
and bag sections
together.

(Below)
Detail of the inside of
the workbag showing
the pincushion.

9 With right sides together, first pin and then machine one of the other strips of calico to the embroidered strip. Machine the two strips together, leaving the seam open between each pair of marks (see Figure 74).

10 With right sides together machine the two remaining strips together, down one long seam, to form the lining.

11 With right sides together pin the lining and the bag sections together along one narrow edge (see Figure 75). Machine in place and trim the seam allowances.

12 With right sides facing, pin the remaining long seam together forming a tube. Machine the seam together,

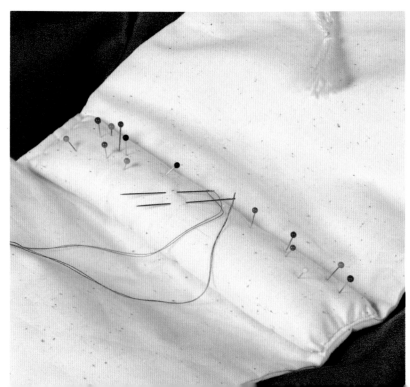

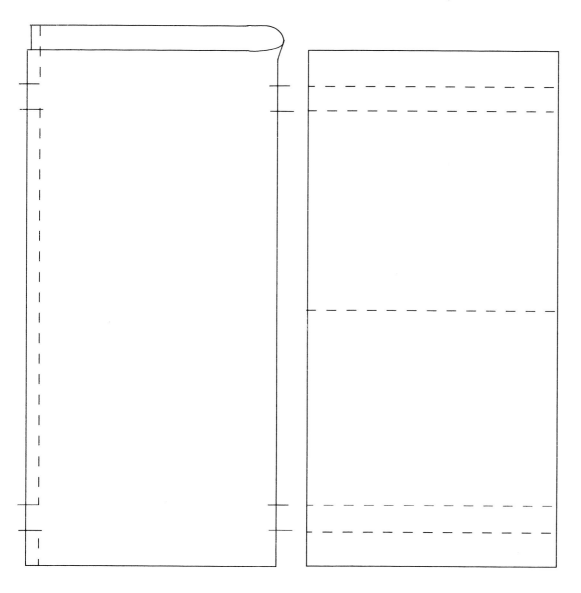

*Fig.76 (far left)
Machine the
remaining long seams
together, so forming a
tube. Leave an
opening between each
of the marked points
as shown.*

*Fig.77 (left)
Mark and machine
across the halfway
point through all
thicknesses of fabric.
Machine two lines of
stitching at each end
of the bag to form cord
channels.*

leaving an opening between each of the marked points (see Figure 76).

13 Pull the lining to the wrong side. Press and turn in the raw edges of the remaining ends of the bag and slip stitch the opening together.

14 Find and mark the halfway point of the tube and machine across through all thicknesses of fabric, thus forming two separate compartments (see Figure 77).

15 To form the channels for the cords at each end of the bag, machine two lines of stitching, 2 cm (¾ in) apart, between the unstitched points. You can make a cord (see General Instructions, page 21) or buy one for each of the two channels.

16 For the pincushion inside the workbag, cut a strip of calico approximately 12 × 21 cm (4¾ × 8½ in) and a piece of wadding approximately 24 × 21 cm (9½ × 8½ in). Turn under and press the raw edges of the calico and wrap it around the folded over piece of wadding. Slip stitch the openings and then stitch the pincushion to the base of the bag, on the inside.

PANEL

The machine embroidered panel of poppies is very straightforward and not at all difficult to work, although you should have some practice at free machining first (see page 78). The background fabric is coloured with green fabric paint and the poppy heads are worked in hand embroidery. The finished size of the panel is 13 × 17 cm (5¼ × 6¾ in).

Materials

- Calico for the background
- Sponge
- Green fabric paint
- Machine embroidery threads in several shades of green, ranging from dark to light
- Dark red hand embroidery thread
- Purchased picture frame

METHOD

1 Cut a piece of calico, or closely woven cotton, approximately 23 × 27 cm (9 × 10½ in).

2 Lay the fabric on a flat surface and dampen it with a wet sponge. Using the sponge apply the fabric paint unevenly over the whole area. Leave to dry and then iron the reverse of the fabric to set the paint.

3 Figure 78 gives only the main lines of the embroidery. Referring to the General Instructions on page 10, transfer the design to the fabric. Alternatively, using the illustration as reference, lightly draw the lines directly on to the fabric in soft pencil.

A field of poppies provided the inspiration for this picture which is worked in green and red embroidery threads.

4 Beginning with a dark green machine embroidery thread, work lines of vertical free machining over the calico (see the Machine embroidery section on page 78). Make the lines bend and curve over each other as you work, so that they resemble foliage.

5 Continue embroidering in this way, machining the lines of stitchery on top of each other, bending and curving and working gradually through to the lightest shade of green.

6 When you feel that you have finished all the machine embroidery, and you are happy with the results, remove the work from the frame and trim the threads. Press the back of the work. (It may need to be damp stretched at this stage — see page 16.)

7 The poppies are simply groups of two or three hand satin stitches (see Figure 19 on page 26), worked in different directions, using a fine, dark red thread. Dot them at random over the green stitchery so that they look as if they are 'growing'.

8 Mount the panel (see General Instructions on page 17).

Fig.78 (left) Transfer this design to the fabric then work vertical lines of free machine embroidery over the calico.

(Right) This panel is not difficult to work. The calico background is coloured with green fabric paint, the stems are machine embroidered and the poppy heads are hand embroidered.

RIBBONS

Satin ribbons and machine embroidery are combined to produce an attractive hardwearing fabric, which is used here to make a jewellery roll and a sewing companion. At the end of this section two pretty Valentine cards are created from left over pieces of fabric, ribbons and metallic threads.

JEWELLERY ROLL

This jewellery roll is beautifully decorated with a combination of ribbons and automatic sewing machine patterns. Satin ribbons of various widths are machined to a background fabric using some of the automatic stitches on a modern sewing machine, although straight running stitch could be used, if you prefer. Choose a good tempered fabric for backing, such as cotton, and select matching or contrasting machine threads for the appliqué.

This jewellery roll is decorated with three different coloured satin ribbons which are applied on to cotton fabric and embellished with a variety of beautiful machine embroidered stitches.

Materials
- 1 m (1 yd) of cotton backing fabric
- A selection of ribbons in four different widths. These were purchased in 2 m (2 yd) lengths
- Matching and contrasting machine sewing cottons
- 20 cm (8 in) zip
- Small piece terylene wadding
- Snap fastener

METHOD

1 Cut a strip of backing fabric 40 × 28 cm (16 × 11 in). Pin the first strip of ribbon in place, tack and machine using a straight stitch, or select an automatic pattern (see Figure 79). The ribbons have been stitched down diagonally on the jewellery roll and care must be taken when stitching, as this tends to pucker the fabric. It is perfectly acceptable to stitch the ribbons in straight rows if you prefer.

2 Pin, tack and stitch the next ribbon in place. Vary the spacing between the rows and the width of each strip of ribbon. Choose two or three different automatic stitches to decorate the fabric but do not be tempted to use too many, or the finished result will look rather messy.

3 When all the ribbons have been stitched down, remove the tacking threads and carefully press the back of the fabric with a steam iron. Trim the fabric to 35 × 22 cm (14 × 8¾ in).

4 Cut two more pieces of fabric to the size 35 × 22 cm (14 × 8¾ in) and a third piece 20 × 22 cm (8 × 8¾ in). These will be used for the lining of the jewellery roll and for the pockets.

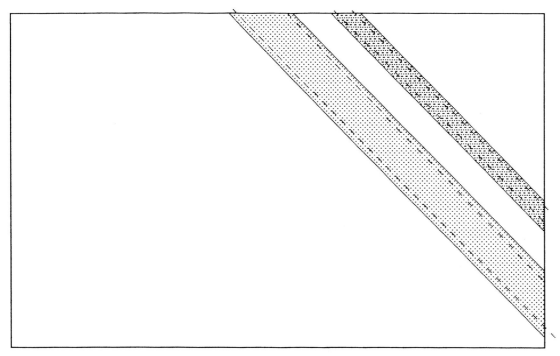

(Right)
Detail of the machine stitching on the jewellery roll. With a limited range of colours and stitches, it is possible to achieve a great number of permutations yet the overall design will still look co-ordinated.

Fig.79 (left)
Pin the ribbon to the backing fabric and machine in place.

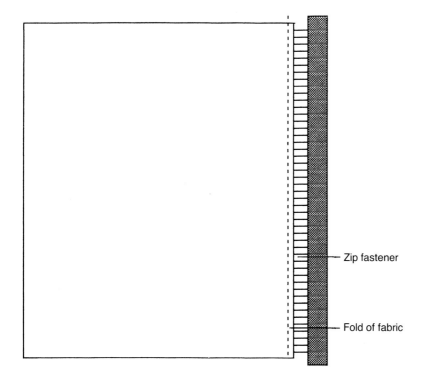

— Zip fastener

— Fold of fabric

Fig.80
Fold and press the fabric wrong sides together. Attach one side of the zip to the folded edge.

5 Fold and press one of the larger pieces of fabric, wrong sides together. Attach one side of the zip to the folded edge (see Figure 80).
6 Lay the other large piece of fabric right side up and find and mark the centre. Place the folded pocket with zip attached over this fabric, with the zip lying face down (see Figure 81). Pin, tack and stitch the second side of the zip to the larger piece of fabric.
7 Pin and tack the raw edges of the pocket to the lining (see Figure 82).
8 For the ring roll, cut a piece of fabric, approximately 17 × 6 cm (6¾ × 2¾ in) and a piece of wadding approximately 40 × 6 cm (16 × 2¾ in). Turn and press a small seam on all four sides. Roll the wadding quite tightly and roll the fabric around the wadding. Slip stitch the edges together.
9 Stitch one end of the ring roll to the pocket, just below the zip, and attach a snap fastener to the other end (see Figure 83).
10 Fold and press the remaining piece of fabric, wrong sides together, and pin

Fig.81
Lay the folded pocket with attached zip over the large piece of fabric and stitch the second side of the zip to this fabric.

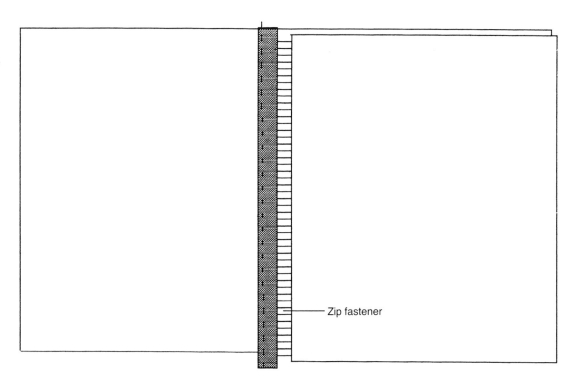

Zip fastener

Fig.82
Tack the raw edges of the pocket to the lining.

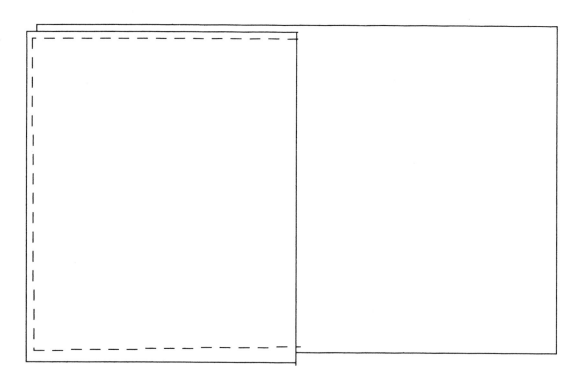

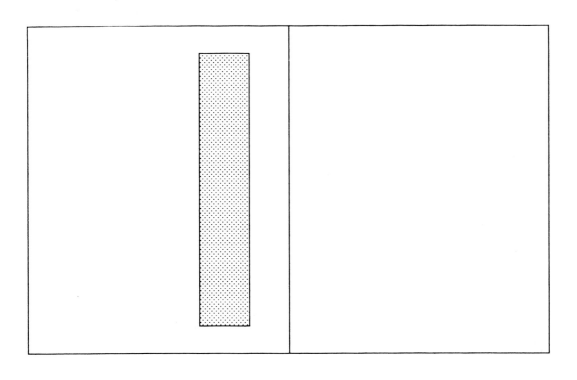

over the large pocket. Tack the edges in place.

11 Divide this piece into three pockets by machining two rows of stitching, 7 cm (3 in) apart, through all the layers of fabric (see Figure 84).

12 Cut a piece of terylene wadding, 35 × 22 cm (14 × 8¾ in) and make a sandwich of lining, wadding and outer fabric. It is helpful at this stage to pin and tack all the layers together (see Figure 82). Slightly round off all four corners.

13 Cut a strip of bias fabric from the remaining fabric (see General Instructions, page 19). Pin to the right side of the jewellery roll and machine.

14 Cut a length of ribbon for the ties and tack to the centre of one narrow side before turning the bias strip to the wrong side. Turn under a narrow hem and slip stitch in place.

The plain-coloured bias binding provides a perfect foil to the richness of the embroidery.

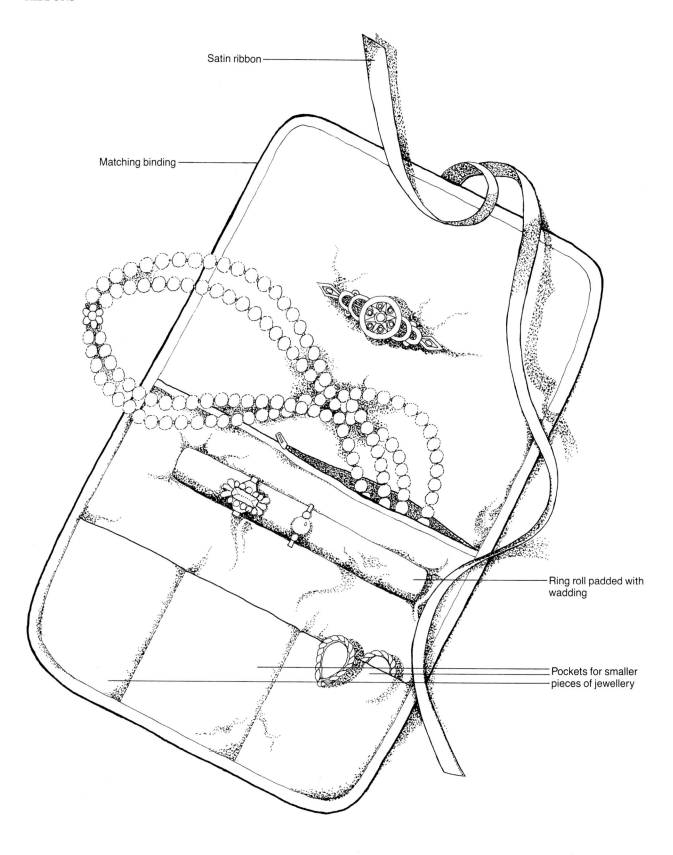

Satin ribbon

Matching binding

Ring roll padded with wadding

Pockets for smaller pieces of jewellery

Fig.84
Attach the folded fabric to the pocket and tack in place. Divide it into three pockets as shown.

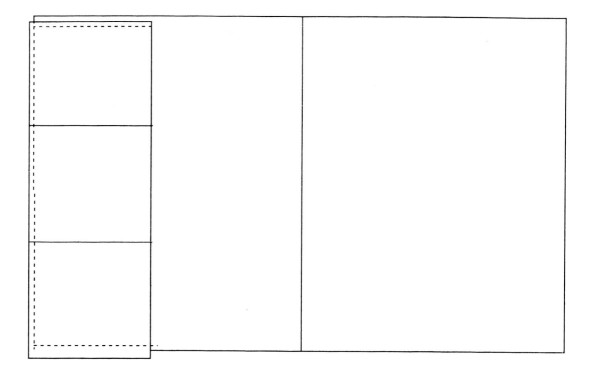

Fig.85
Cut a piece of wadding and make a sandwich of lining, wadding and outer fabric. Tack all the layers together.

(Left)
The inside of the jewellery roll.

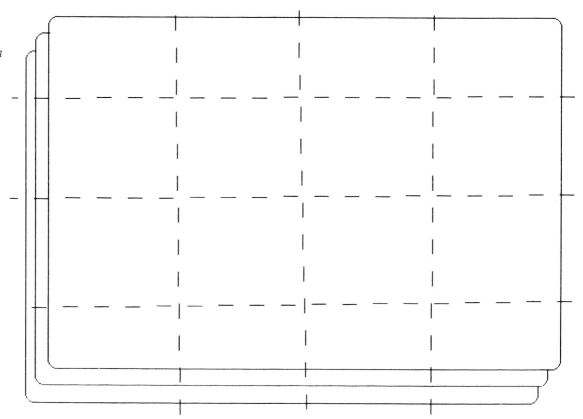

SEWING COMPANION

The instructions for this sewing companion were discovered in the 'Needlecraft Monthly Magazine', dated December 1912. Velvet ribbon was specified but a good quality cotton fabric is used here. The pincushion and pocket are decorated with ribbons left over from the jewellery roll project.

Materials

- 25 cm (10 in) cotton fabric
- Pelmet Vilene
- Ribbons for decoration
- Sewing cotton to match fabric
- Filling for pincushion (wadding)
- Length of narrow ribbon to attach scissors

Fig.86
Turn a 1 cm (⅜ in)
hem on the two long
edges.

The sewing
companion is worn
around the neck and
hangs down on either
side, with the
pincushion on one
side and the scissors
on the other.

METHOD

1 Cut a strip of fabric 90 × 12 cm (36 × 4¾ in) and a strip of Vilene 92 × 5 cm (36 × 2 in).

2 Turn under and press to the wrong side a 1 cm (⅜ in) hem on the two long edges of the fabric (see Figure 86). With the wrong sides together press the fabric in half lengthways so that the two folded edges meet in the centre. Insert the strip of Vilene into the fabric strip and pin the layers together (see Figure 87).

3 Machine two rows of stitching on each side of the centre fold, ending the stitching about 2 cm (¾ in) before the ends on each side. Stitch again along the outer folded edges, again ending the stitching about 2 cm (¾ in) before the ends (see Figure 88).

4 Turn under a narrow hem on one of the remaining raw edges. Cut a length of ribbon, approximately 36 cm (14 in) and thread through the handle of a pair of embroidery scissors. Tuck the ends of the ribbon well into the long strip of fabric and slip stitch the edges together.

5 For the pincushion, cut two squares of fabric 10 × 10 cm (4 × 4 in). Decorate one piece with ribbons in the same manner described for the jewellery roll.

6 Place the two squares of fabric right sides together, and machine around three sides. Turn to the right side and press well before stuffing with wadding.

7 Turn in the raw edges on the remaining side. Insert the other end of the long strip into the pincushion and carefully slip stitch the edges together (see Figure 89).

8 Make a pocket by cutting two strips of fabric 7.5 × 7 cm (3 × 2¾ in). Decorate one piece with ribbons.

9 Place the two pieces of fabric right sides together and machine around three sides. Turn to the right side and press well. Turn in the raw edges and slip stitch them together.

10 Pin the pocket to the long machined strip, just above the pincushion, and slip stitch in place.

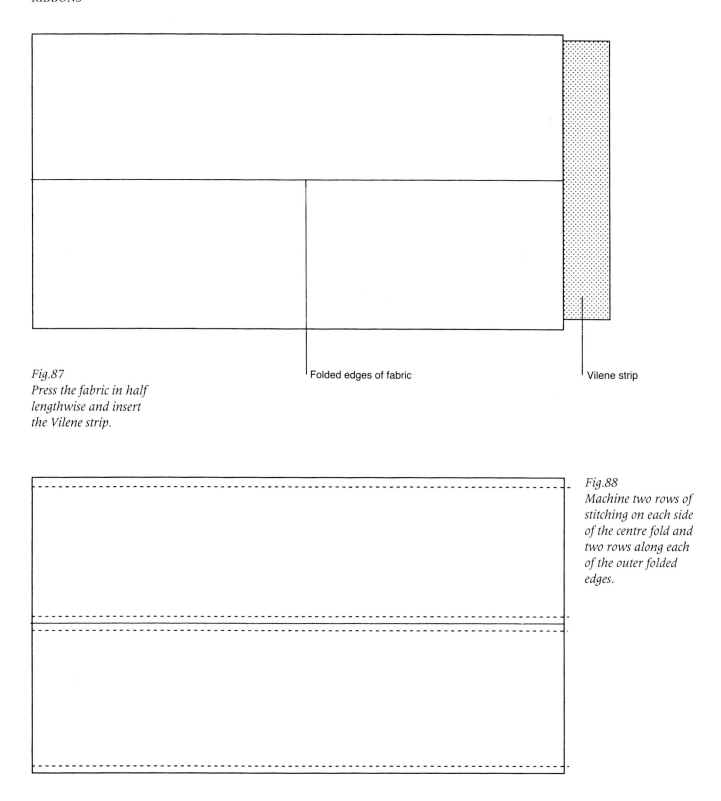

Fig.87
Press the fabric in half lengthwise and insert the Vilene strip.

Folded edges of fabric

Vilene strip

Fig.88
Machine two rows of stitching on each side of the centre fold and two rows along each of the outer folded edges.

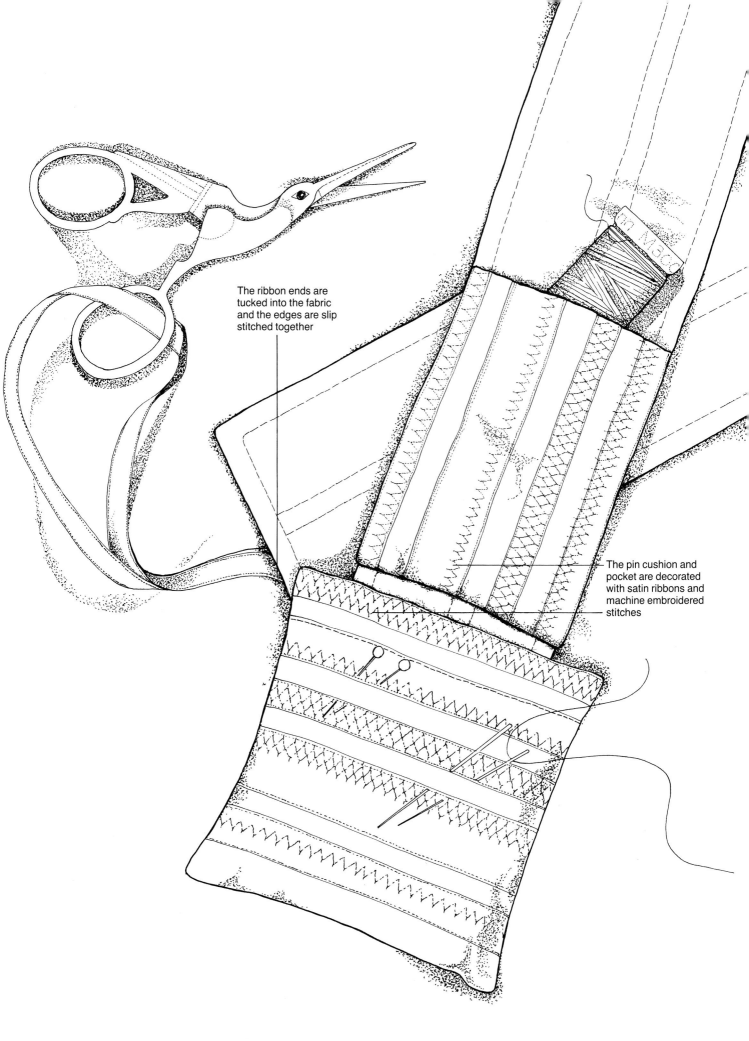

The ribbon ends are tucked into the fabric and the edges are slip stitched together

The pin cushion and pocket are decorated with satin ribbons and machine embroidered stitches

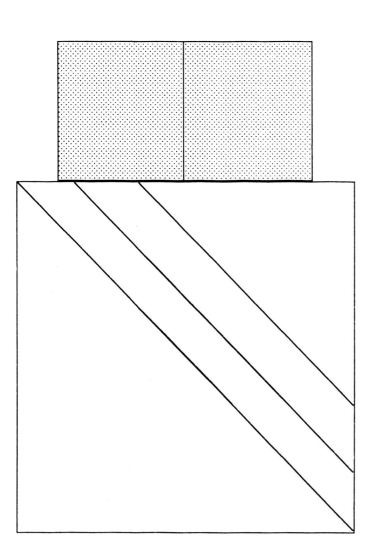

Fig.89
*Attach the pincushion
to one end of the long
strip of fabric.*

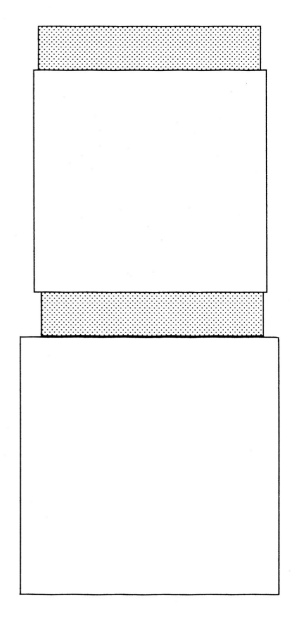

Fig.90
*Attach the pocket to
the strip just above the
pincushion.*

VALENTINE CARDS

These were made with left over fabrics and mounted in purchased greetings card blanks with an aperture in the shape of a heart.

Materials

- Card
- Calico
- Left over fabrics
- Ribbon
- Metallic threads
- Embroidery threads

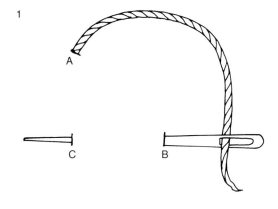

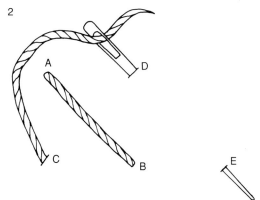

Fig.91
Cross stitch. *This is traditionally worked on an evenweave fabric but it looks equally effective worked on finer fabrics. 1. Bring the needle out of the fabric at A, insert at B and bring out again at C. 2. From C re-insert the needle at D and bring out again at E ready to start the next stitch.*

The card on the left contains strips of different coloured silks, cut on the bias with pinking shears, and some ribbons from the jewellery roll. The card on the right is made from a piece of silk patchwork.

(Right)
Use left over pieces of fabric and ribbon to make your own personal Valentine cards. This is one occasion when you can go over the top with colour and decoration.

Fig.92
Draw the heart outline on to the calico.

METHOD

Mount a small piece of calico in a hoop and draw the outline of the card aperture on to the calico using an HB pencil. Arrange pieces of fabric over the calico until you have achieved an interesting design. Both cards are decorated with simple hand stitchery – running stitch (see Figure 22 on page 29), cross stitch (see Figure 91) and couched metallic threads (see Figure 93).

Remove the embroidery from the hoop and trim away the excess fabric. Lightly press the back of the work. Centre the embroidery over the card aperture and hold in place with sellotape. Lightly glue the backing in place and leave to dry.

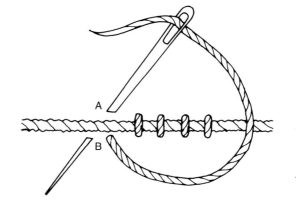

Fig.93
Couching. *This is used to hold down metallic and other interesting threads that would be difficult to stitch into the fabric. Lay the metallic thread across the surface of the fabric. With the needle threaded using a fine matching or contrasting coloured thread, insert it into the fabric at A and bring out again at B. The stitches should be at right angles to the couched thread.*

$\mathcal{S}$TARS

The inspiration for the book cover and quilted cushion came from a furnishing fabric printed with a design of gold stars, and from a small piece of striped silk fabric in shades of red and purple.

BOOK COVER

A rich purple silk was used for the book cover but a furnishing fabric in any dark colour would be suitable. Although the embroidery was worked on a striped fabric, a piece of plain silk or rich fabric in a contrasting colour could equally well be used.

This book cover fits an A5 book, but measure your chosen book very accurately in case the measurements vary slightly.

Materials
- 50 cm (½ yd) of silk or furnishing fabric (this will be enough for both the cushion and the book cover)
- Piece of contrasting silk for the embroidered inset, approximately 18 × 12 cm (7 × 4½ in)
- 50 cm (½ yd) calico
- 50 cm (½ yd) fusible adhesive webbing
- 50 cm (½ yd) fabric for lining (cotton would be suitable)
- Gold fabric paint
- Selection of embroidery threads in matching colours (turquoise, red, purple and pink are used here, but your choice will depend on your colour scheme)
- Metallic thread

The rich colours of the silk fabrics and the gold star motif give these two projects an exotic oriental feel. The book cover would make a diary or day book very special.

METHOD

The embroidered inset is worked first, before starting on the whole cover.

EMBROIDERED INSET

1 Transfer the design in Figure 94 to the inset fabric using the tracing and tacking method (see page 13).
2 Cut a piece of fusible adhesive webbing the same size as the backing fabric. Lay the tacky side of the webbing on the wrong side of the fabric. Press with a hot iron until both pieces are firmly glued together. Peel off the paper backing fabric and lay the fabric, sticky side down, on to a piece of calico. Press both fabrics firmly together.
3 Place the fabrics in an embroidery hoop. It is not necessary to stick rigidly to the same order as Figure 94; the small triangles and the stars could be moved around, and other couched threads could be used if desired.
4 Work the triangles first in satin stitch (see Figure 19 on page 26); use the same colour throughout one row, but vary the colours from row to row.
5 Using a fine metallic thread, stitch the tiny triangles in back stitch (see Figure 18 on page 26). Stitch one row of stars in metallic thread and the other row in normal embroidery thread. The stars are

back stitches worked on top of each other (see Figure 95).

6 Couch down the metallic threads beneath the triangles (see Figure 93) and add a few rows of running stitch (see Figure 22 on page 29) to finish the design.

COVER

The star pattern on the fabric was printed using a potato. Alternatively a star-shaped piece of card could be cut out and glued to the end of a cotton reel to make a block.

1 Cut a piece of backing fabric, 55 × 30 cm (21½ × 11½ in).

2 To make the printing block cut a potato in half; transfer the star shape to the cut side by making a template and drawing round the design (see Figure 93). Cut away the potato from around the star.

3 Place the fabric face up on a flat surface with two or three newspapers beneath it. Brush the gold fabric paint on to the potato star and stamp it firmly on the fabric. The pattern was printed randomly throughout the fabric and looks very effective when used this way.

4 Leave the paint to dry, then iron the fabric on the wrong side for several minutes to set the colour.

5 Using fusible adhesive webbing, bond the fabric to a piece of calico the same size (refer to the embroidered inset for instructions).

6 At this stage you will need to take careful measurements of the book you intend to cover. The inset, measuring 8 × 15 cm (3¼ × 6 in) should be centred on the front cover. This will be on the right hand side of the fabric, but remember to allow for the flaps on either side (see Figure 97). Using a soft pencil, centre and mark the inset on the fabric. Cut away the excess fabric, leaving a turning of approximately 1.5 cm (½ in) all around. Snip carefully into the corners and fold the turnings back

(see Figure 98). Press and tack them in place.

7 Lay the embroidered inset in the space, ensuring that the rows of stitching are horizontal. Tack in place and hem stitch (see Figure 31 on page 36) the inset to the backing fabric (see Figure 99). Remove all the tacking threads.

8 To make up the book cover, mark the dimensions of the book on the right side of the fabric making sure that the embroidered inset is in the middle of the front cover. This can be done with tailor's chalk or tacking stitches.

Fig.94
Transfer the design on to the fabric.

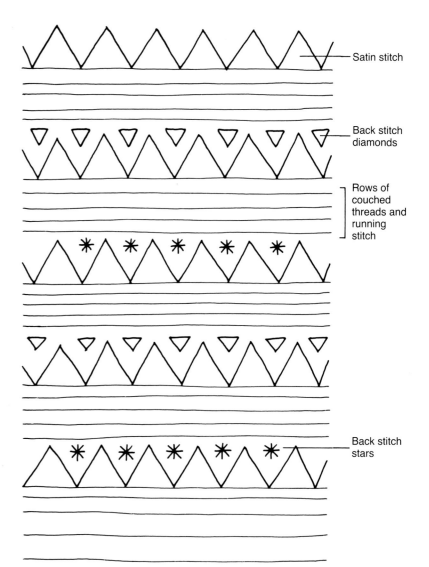

Satin stitch

Back stitch diamonds

Rows of couched threads and running stitch

Back stitch stars

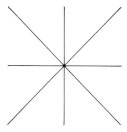

Fig.95
The stars are made by working back stitches on top of one another.

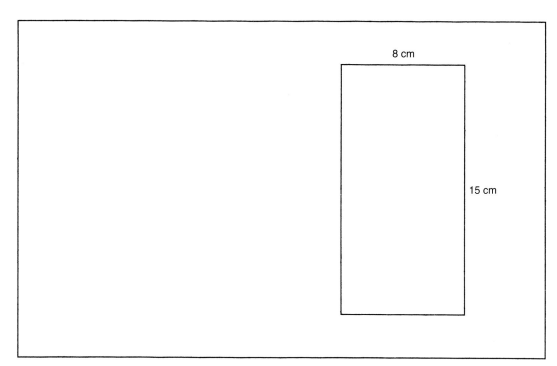

8 cm

15 cm

Fig.96
Transfer the star shape to the potato to make a printing block.

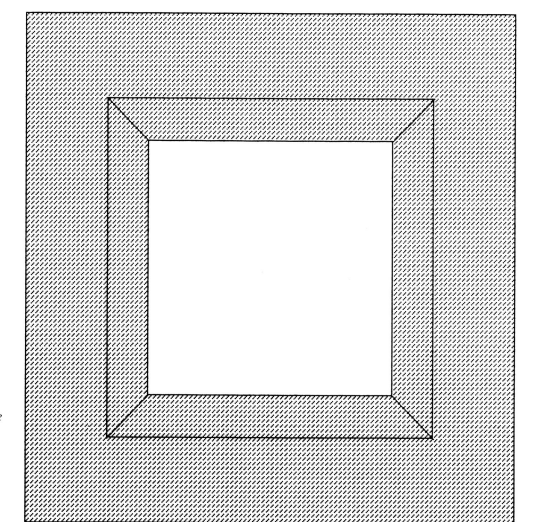

Fig.97 (top right)
Centre the inset on the front cover.

Fig.98 (bottom right)
Press and tack the turnings in place.

9 Cut a piece of lining fabric to match the size of the printed fabric. Place the two pieces right sides together and machine around the marked line, leaving an opening in one side. Turn the fabrics right side out and slip stitch the opening.

10 Place the cover over the book then turn and pin the flap sections in place. Slip stitch them carefully at top and bottom edges.

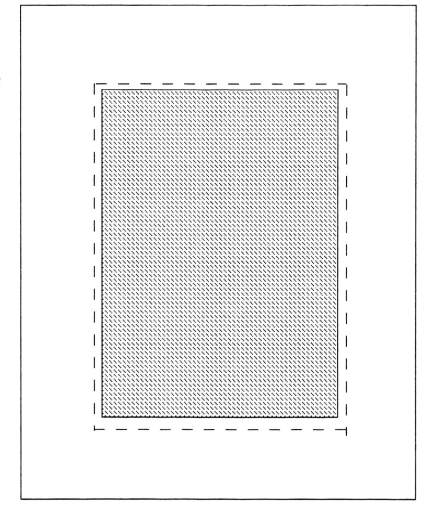

Fig.99 (right)
Attach the inset to the
backing fabric using
hem stitch.

Fig.100 (below)
Mark the dimensions
of the book on the
right side of the fabric.

(Left)
Close-up of the inset
panel on the book
cover. The tiny
embroidered stars
echo the printed gold
stars on the
background fabric.
Couched metallic
threads add to the
texture and richness of
this design.

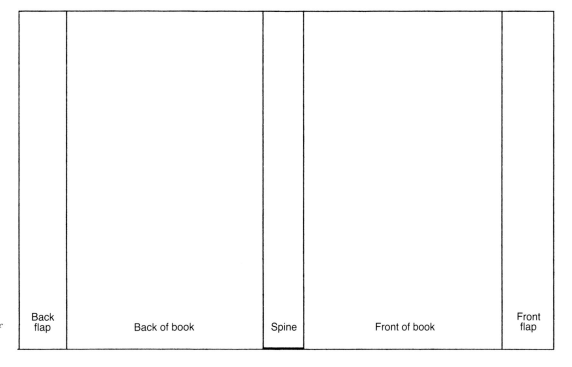

Back flap · Back of book · Spine · Front of book · Front flap

CUSHION

The small quilted cushion is made with the same fabrics as the book cover. This time the inset is printed with gold stars and the surrounding fabric is left plain.

METHOD

1 Print the stars on the cushion centre, following the instructions given above.

> ### Materials
> - 50 cm (½ yd) silk fabric
> - 20 × 20 cm (8 × 8 in) contrasting silk for cushion centre
> - Gold fabric paint
> - 20 × 20 cm (8 × 8 in) of 2 oz wadding
> - 20 × 20 cm (8 × 8 in) butter muslin for backing
> - Piping cord
> - Quilting thread in matching colour

This time, however, the stars are printed in a regular pattern instead of a random design.

2 Cut two strips of the contrasting fabric 20 × 8 cm (8 × 3 in) and two strips 36 × 8 cm (14 × 3 in).

3 Sew the shorter strips to two opposite sides of the cushion centre; press and turn the strips back.

4 Sew the longer strips of fabric to the remaining two sides.

5 Take the square of butter muslin and square of wadding. Lay the muslin on a flat surface, place the wadding on top and the cushion fabric on top of the wadding. Tack all three layers together. Using small running stitches (see Figure 22 on page 29), quilt around each star and around the edge of the cushion centre. For more detailed quilting instructions refer to page 28.

6 Make up the cushion as shown in the General Instructions on page 21, including a piped edge.

The centre panel of the cushion is quilted around each of the printed gold stars, which throws them into relief very effectively.

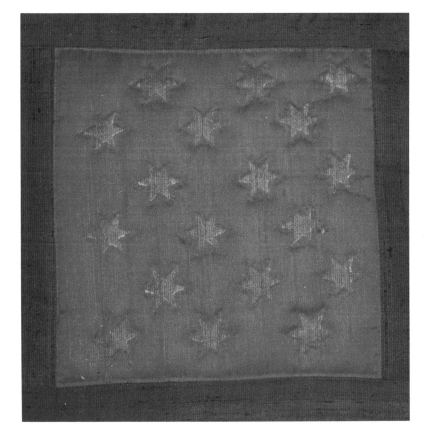

POT POURRI BAGS

The pretty bag on the right was made with offcuts of the printed fabric. Pot pourri bags are made by simply folding a rectangle of fabric in half, with the right sides together. Turn under and stitch the top edge.

Fill the bags with pot pourri mixture or dried lavender and secure with a twisted cord and tassel. They could also be used as tiny gift bags.

Small pieces of left over fabric are ideal for pot pourri or lavender bags, fastened with a contrast cord. The star motif appears again as a freely interpreted design on a greetings card.

CELTIC DESIGNS

A pattern first discovered on an ancient Celtic cross is used for the cushion and a similar pattern is used to decorate the richly coloured bag, which could be used as a sewing bag, or a jewellery bag.

CUSHION

The complicated intertwining Celtic designs, like these shown here, make excellent patterns for quilting. English or wadded quilting is used for this particular cushion design and it is worked in a rich, burnt orange silk. However, the designs would be equally effective in Italian corded quilting.

Materials

- 50 cm (½ yd) fabric, preferably one with a sheen
- Matching quilting thread
- 50 cm (½ yd) of 2 oz terylene wadding
- 50 cm (½ yd) butter muslin

This stunning cushion shows that quilted designs can look just as good in bold colours, as well as the more traditional cream or white. Even a dark colour such as navy would work well.

METHOD

1 Figure 101 is one quarter of the whole design. Trace the pattern on to a large sheet of tracing paper and then repeat the design three times to complete it. Take care to reverse the design as shown (see Figure 102) or the interlaced lines will not work.

2 Transfer the design to the fabric (see General Instructions on page 10).

3 Cut a square of butter muslin and wadding, the same size as the top fabric. Place the muslin on a flat surface and cover with the wadding. Place the top fabric over the wadding and smooth in place. Tack all three layers together.

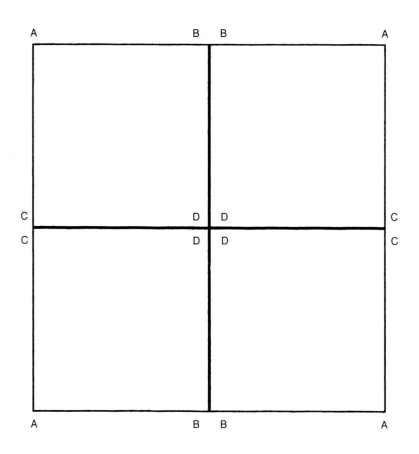

Fig.101
Repeat the design three times, reversing it as shown.

Fig.102
Trace the design on to a large sheet of tracing paper.

Refer to the section on Quilting for more detailed instructions (see page 28).

4 Using running stitches (see Figure 22 on page 29), quilt the lines of the design. When all the design has been worked, quilt a straight line around the edge of the pattern and leave an unquilted strip approximately 2.5 cm (1 in) beyond this line to form a border around the edge of the cushion.

5 Make up the cushion (see General Instructions on page 18), including a piped edge.

BAG

Rich silks are used to make this bag, but any smooth fabric would be appropriate. The designs are applied to the fabric with machine stitching.

Materials

- 50 cm (½ yd) fabric
- 50 cm (½ yd) lining fabric
- Six strips of contrasting fabric 30 cm (12 in) long and 9 cm (3½ in) wide
- Contrasting machine sewing thread
- Fusible adhesive webbing
- Matching cord or ribbon for ties

Here a bold Celtic pattern is used as a dramatic contrast to the background fabric. The piping round the top of the bag makes a nice finishing touch.

METHOD

1 Using tracing or greaseproof paper, trace off the Celtic pattern, noting that the design is in two sections (see Figures 103 and 104). Place the fusible adhesive webbing, paper side up, over the design for the traced drawing, and trace off the pattern six times.

2 Place the fusible adhesive webbing over the contrasting fabric and iron firmly in place. Do not remove the paper backing. Using small sharp scissors, carefully cut away all the shapes between the interlacing lines, taking great care not to cut the pattern lines.

3 From the bag fabric, cut a strip 57 cm (22½ in) long and 32 cm (12½ in) wide. Peel the backing paper away from the bonded strips and arrange them face up on the right side of the fabric. Place a sheet of silicone paper over them and iron firmly in place.

4 Using a sewing thread in a contrasting colour, switch rows of machine stitching just inside the edges of each line, continuing the stitching line for as far as possible before fastening off. The lines of stitchery will overlap each other and form an important part of the design.

Fig.103 (left)
Trace off the design, lightly marking points A and B.

Fig.104 (right)
Place this below Figure 103 matching points A and B, and trace off the design.

5 To make up the bag, cut a strip of lining fabric the same size as the outer bag. (This could be the same fabric, as illustrated here, or a contrast).

6 Place the bag and lining fabrics right sides together and machine along the top of the bag. (A narrow strip of piping is inserted into the seam before it is stitched together, but this is not essential.) Trim the seam allowances.

7 With right sides together, pin and machine the bag and lining together along the long seam, so forming a tube.

8 For the base, cut a circle 16 cm (6¼ in) diameter from the outer bag fabric, and one the same size from the lining.

9 With right sides together, pin, tack and machine the circular base to the base of the outer bag. Clip the seam.

10 Turn the bag inside out and carefully press the lining in place. Slip stitch the lining base in place, hiding all the raw edges.

11 Use a twisted cord or length of ribbon to secure the bag.

Detail of the Celtic pattern. The lines of machine stitching are worked in a contrast colour to give an additional dimension to the design. The clever use of a few co-ordinating colours is very effective.

CHRISTMAS

Small embroidered cards and panels worked in festive colours and metallic threads add a seasonal sparkle to Christmas.

Handmade Christmas cards make lovely gifts in their own right and mean so much more than anything you can buy in a shop. The embroidered panel will quickly become part of the traditional family Christmas decorations.

Figs.105, 106, 107 Use these designs as guidelines to refer to while printing on the fabric.

CARDS

These small cards are made from scraps of bright silk fabrics and mounted in purchased greetings card blanks. They are made quickly and quite simply, and they could be further decorated with beads and sequins if desired.

METHOD

1 Using gold fabric paint, print a simple design on each piece of fabric (see page 110 for instructions on how to apply the paint). In these cards, the star is printed with a purchased rubber stamp found in a toy shop. The printed lines are made

Materials

- Purchased greetings card blanks
- Small pieces of brightly coloured silk fabrics, which should be slightly larger than the aperture on the card
- Gold fabric paint
- Purchased rubber stamp in the form of a star
- Two or three embroidery threads in contrasting colours

with the edge of a spare piece of mounting card. The dots on the purple card are dotted on with a paint brush loaded with gold paint (see Figures 105,

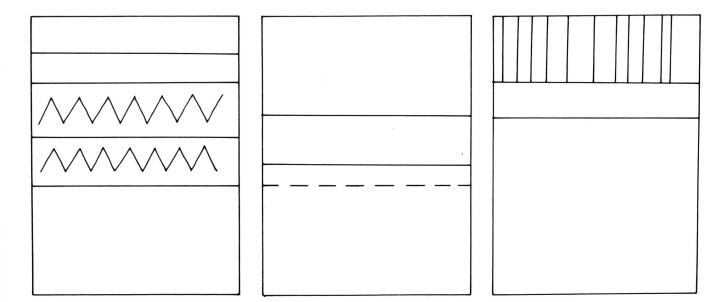

106 and 107). The brush should be carefully washed after it has been used.

2 Leave the paint to dry and iron the wrong side of the fabric to set the design. If the silk fabric is particularly small or thin, it would be advisable at this stage to back it with calico or sheeting.

3 Use simple embroidery stitches and contrasting coloured thread to decorate the cards. Here the stitches used are running stitch (see Figure 22 on page 29), back stitch (see Figure 18 on page 26), cross stitch (see Figure 91 on page 105) and seeding stitch (see Figure 20 on page 26); the cross stitch and seeding stitch are worked in a fine metallic machine embroidery thread which is equally suitable for hand embroidery.

4 Trim away the spare fabric and place the embroidery inside the card, securing it with small pieces of sellotape (see Figure 108). Use adhesive to glue the inset in place.

Fig.108
Place the embroidery inside the card, securing it with sellotape.

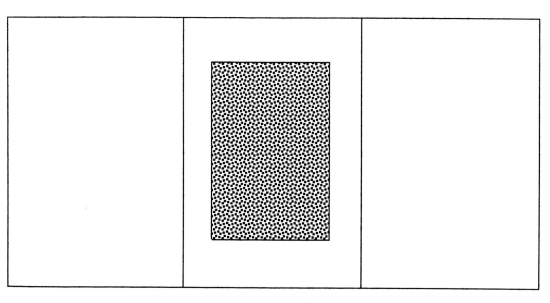

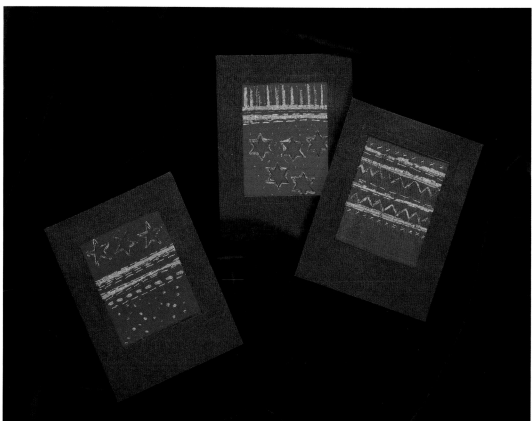

Gold fabric paint and richly coloured silk fabrics conjure up the spirit of Christmas. The simple embroidery stitches add texture and interest, and of course each card is unique.

PANEL

A similar design to the cards is used for the miniature panel. Although it is not particularly intended as a seasonal decoration it could be kept especially for Christmas and brought out each year. The design would also be suitable for a box lid or as an insertion in a small decorative cushion (see page 114 for instructions).

The panel is made in the same way as the cards. A piece of red and blue shot silk has been used so that the colour changes according to the direction of the light. Gold fabric paint and the edge of a piece of mounting card are again used to print the patterns.

The embroidery stitches are back stitch (see Figure 18 on page 26) and running stitch (see Figure 22 on page 29), but with the addition of three rows of couched gold metallic thread (see Figure 93 on page 106).

A small gilt frame was purchased in which to mount the embroidery (see General Instructions on page 17 for mounting and framing work).

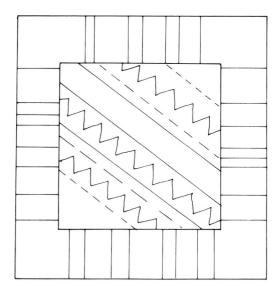

Fig.109
Use this illustration as a guide for the fabric printing.

Close-up of the panel, showing the stitches in detail. The idea is the same as for the Christmas cards, but with the addition of couched gold metallic thread.

ACKNOWLEDGEMENTS

The publishers would like to thank the following for the loan of furniture and props for the photographs in this book.

Special thanks are due to Margaret Seale of **Sealecraft**, Camden Road, Tunbridge Wells, Kent, for her help in supplying threads and materials throughout the book; Gillie Brown for supplying fabrics; Colin Springett, **Up Country Antiques**, The Old Corn Stores, 68 St Johns Road, Tunbridge Wells, Kent, for the loan of the wooden chest on page 34 and the chest and plate on page 89; Jeron Markies, **Aspidistra Antiques**, 16 Hartfield Road, Forest Row, Sussex, for the loan of the silver photograph frames and the crystal decanter on page 67, the pearl necklaces on page 117, the jewellery on page 92 and the picture on page 122.

Thanks are also due to The Architectural Emporium, Tunbridge Wells, for the loan of the fireplace on page 122; Arthur Hayes Opticians, East Grinstead, for the spectacles on page 108; C & H Fabrics, Tunbridge Wells, for the furnishing fabrics on pages 50, 67, 108 and 117; Casafina, Tunbridge Wells, for the furniture and vase on page 43; The Complete Cook, Forest Row, for the coffee set and scissors on page 43; Country Antiques, Tunbridge Wells, for the side table on page 67; Daisy Chain, East Grinstead, for the flower arrangements on pages 67 and 50; First Impressions, Forest Row, for the silver frame containing the lavender panel on page 67; Georgia Stratton, Lewes, for toys and the rocking horse on page 34; Martells, East Grinstead, for the carpet on page 34; John Lewis, London and branches, for the jewellery (from a selection) on page 98; The Oriental Rug Shop, Tunbridge Wells, for the rug on page 108; The Pine Market, Tunbridge Wells, for toys on page 34; and Porcupine, Tunbridge Wells, for the wooden bathroom fittings on page 25.

BIBLIOGRAPHY

Iain Bain, *Celtic Knotwork*, Constable, 1986

Juliet Bawden, *The Art and Craft of Appliqué*, Mitchell Beazley, 1991

Jan Beaney and Jean Littlejohn, *A Complete Guide to Creative Embroidery*, Century, 1991

Thomasina Beck, *The Embroiderer's Garden*, David & Charles, 1988

Jenny Bullen, *The Book of Embroidery Stitches*, A & C Black, 1990

Valerie Campbell-Harding, *Fabric Painting for Embroidery*, B T Batsford, 1990

The Practical Study Group, *Needlework School*, Chartwell Books, 1984

The Practical Study Group, *Embroidery Studio*, David & Charles, 1993

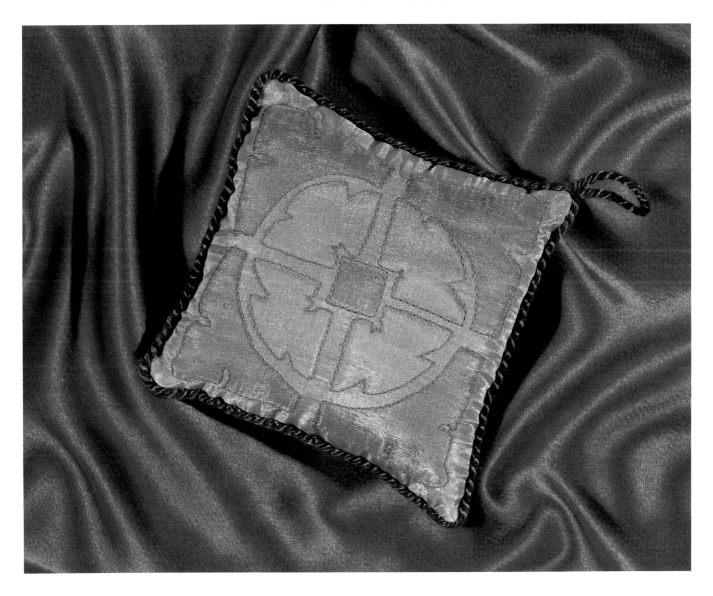

*I*NDEX